Eureka!

Eureka!

Discovering American English and Culture through Proverbs, Fables, Myths, and Legends

Planaria J. Price

Ann Arbor

THE UNIVERSITY OF MICHIGAN PRESS

To the memory of my father, Harold Price, who first showed me the glory of discovery with these stories. With deepest love I thank him for teaching me to "Count that day lost in which you have not learned anything new."

Acknowledgments

This book would not have been written without the enthusiastic support and brilliant editing of Kelly Sippell and the University of Michigan Press. To my delightful illustrator, Xavier Urquieta, I am indebted for putting perfectly into art what I had envisioned and for reading my mind; to Ruth Ryan for her daily cartoon clippings above and beyond the call of friendship; to Sandy Avolevan, whose magic fingers soothed my computer-racked neck and arms; to Larry Brooks, for being there; and, always, to Murray, for being more patient and faithful than Penelope while I abandoned him for the computer to make this grand Odyssey.

Contents

A Parable for *Eureka!*

Once upon a time in ancient Sicily, in the third century B.C., there lived a Greek man named Archimedes (ark-a-me-des). Archimedes was a very famous mathematician and a philosopher. He was always asking why and trying to figure things out. One day, King Hiero of Syracuse asked Archimedes to find out if his new crown was really made out of a pound of pure gold. King Hiero had given a pound of gold to a jeweler to make a crown, but the king did not trust him and suspected that the jeweler had stolen some of the gold and had replaced the gold with silver (which was much cheaper and more common).

Archimedes did not know how to test this because the crown did weigh one pound. He went home and took a bath and thought about the problem. Suddenly, the answer came to him. As usual, when he got into the full tub, some water spilled over onto the floor. Archimedes suddenly realized a scientific fact—that a body (matter) will displace itself in water. He knew that a pound of silver had less mass than a pound of gold and knew he could test the purity of the crown by weighing it in water. Archimedes was so excited that he jumped out of the bath and ran down the city streets to tell the king. He was shouting, "Eureka, Eureka!" (I have found it!) as he ran. He was so delighted with his scientific discovery that he forgot to put on any clothes! Since Archimedes was able to prove that the jeweler was indeed a cheat, nobody seemed to mind that Archimedes ran naked to the king.

Today, when Americans discover something exciting, they say, "Eureka!" but they usually keep their clothes on. "Eureka!" is also the motto of the state of California because of all the gold that was discovered in the state.

As an ESL student, you know the value of adding more English to your life. Now, all you have to do is open the pages of this book and say, "Eureka!" and you will discover exciting new ways to add to your knowledge of American English, idioms, and culture. These discoveries can be made in your classroom, at a desk, or even in your bath without your clothes. And you, like Archimedes, will become rich and successful with the valuable knowledge of what you have found.

Introduction to the Teacher
and the Student

Why?

Once, in ancient Greece, there was a king of Corinth whose name was Sisyphus /sis-uh-fuss/. One day he saw a giant eagle kidnap a young woman and carry her away to a distant island. Sisyphus suspected that the eagle was Zeus, the king of the gods. In mythology, the gods often took on animal shapes or forms. When King Sisyphus told the young woman's father what he had seen, he was accused of betraying a secret of Zeus. For that crime, Zeus punished Sisyphus in a most horrible way. He sent the unfortunate king to Hades (hell) and made him roll a large rock up a steep hill. Just as the rock reaches the top, it slips from Sisyphus's grasp, and Sisyphus is doomed to keep trying to roll it back up the hill for eternity.

Do you see any similarity between the troubles of Sisyphus and his rock and yourself and English? *Students,* do you feel that you will never achieve the fluency you need? Are you studying hard and learning, and yet English is still a heavy load? *Teachers,* are you feeling the frustration of teaching the best you can, and yet finding that there are still great gaps in your students' communicative competence?

This book was written to help both teachers and students push that rolling rock of English over the top of that steep hill or mountain of frustration so that you will soon see the difficulties of understanding and communicating in English roll easily away.

How?

Since a language is a system of sounds to communicate meanings, and since the meanings—the ideas—come from one's culture, it stands to reason that one cannot learn a language without learning the culture of that language *at the same time.* American English is filled with vocabulary, idioms, allusions, and cultural values from the ancient Western world. The stories, art, and ideals of ancient Greece and Rome and of England during the Middle Ages and the Renaissance have greatly influenced the language and culture of modern American English. It follows that knowledge of the most famous of those stories will greatly enhance the language abilities of the ESL learner. To truly learn a second language the student must find the learning to be relevant and fun. The material in *Eureka!* is both meaningful and enjoyable. *Eureka!* offers the best-known proverbs, fables, myths, and classical English legends. All the fables, myths, and legends in *Eureka!* have considered the literary styles and moral lessons from the original sources but they have all been retold for the non-English-speaking reader. Reading *Eureka!* will aid students in the joyful discovery of American English by adding to their knowledge of vocabulary and idioms, increasing their reading skills, and most of all, introducing them to the most famous of the proverbs and moral lessons that have influenced modern American culture.

Using This Book

This book is designed to further your enjoyment of reading, improve your reading skills, enlarge your vocabulary and teach you how to figure out clues to solving the mysteries of American idioms and culture. Following are some of the methods in *Eureka!* to help you achieve those goals.

Reading Readiness: Before you begin each story there will be clues about that story hiding in an advertisement, cartoon, or advice column. You will be asked to guess what you think the story will be about. *You are not expected to know the correct answers.* Sometimes you might feel confused. This activity is designed to be fun and to polish your skills at guessing. When you finish each story, be sure to look at the "reading readiness" again. You will be surprised and delighted at how easy it will now be for you to find all the hidden clues and to now understand the total meaning of the exercise.

Proverbs: At the end of each story in this book, you will see three famous American proverbs and be asked to choose which proverb you think best fits the moral of the story. In almost every case, there will be no one right answer! Your choice might depend on your culture and its system of values, or it might depend on your point of view about the story. For instance: a famous American proverb is "the squeaky wheel gets the oil." That means that you must take care of yourself and speak up—those who complain the loudest will get the most attention. This is generally considered to be a positive trait in the United States, but in other cultures this trait is not positive. Instead, you may have been taught "the nail that stands higher gets hit first." That means that you should be quiet and try not to stand out in a crowd. Because of these types of cultural differences, you will have very interesting and enlightening conversations with your classmates about which proverb best teaches the lesson of the story. After *you* decide which proverb *you* think is the best one, be sure to turn to pages 196–99 in the back of the book and check that proverb off.

Because most proverbs use an older language and have specific cultural meanings, they are often difficult to understand. To clarify the American meanings of the proverbs, definitions are given in that section of the book.

Vocabulary from Fables, Myths, and Legends: In addition to the new everyday vocabulary words you will learn in each chapter, there will be special words, phrases, and idioms that come directly from the fables, mythology, and legends that you read. (Simple pronunciation guidelines are given for some names.) Be sure to turn to page 207 and keep adding to that list. You will be amazed at how many new words you have discovered when you finish this book and that you have created your own personal dictionary of new words.

A Brief History of the English Language

More than 300 million people in the world speak English and the rest, it sometimes seems, try to.
—Bill Bryson, *The Mother Tongue: English and How It Got That Way* (1990)

The English language is the sea which receives tributaries from every region under heaven.
—Ralph Waldo Emerson (1803–82)

We are walking lexicons. In a single sentence of idle chatter we preserve Latin, Anglo-Saxon, Norse; we carry a museum inside our heads, each day we commemorate peoples of whom we have never heard.
—Penelope Lively, *Moon Tiger* (1988)

You probably don't know this, and you probably won't agree at first, but you have chosen to learn, as your second language, one of the most important languages in today's world. English is important because more than 300 million people speak English as their native language and another 350 million people, plus **you**, speak it as their second language. Half of the world's books are published in English; it is the official language for all air travel; and 80 percent of computer texts are written in English.

English is also one of the easiest languages to learn—*as a second language.* "So why am I struggling!!?" you ask. If you think English is hard to learn, it's because learning any second language, as an adult, is hard to do. One of the secrets to learning English quickly is to not expect English to work the same way your first language works; English has its own set of rules.

Another secret is to relax and figure out the patterns, and then you'll see how truly easy English can be. Learning a new language is like playing a game. Just learn the patterns and rules and soon you will win!

You may think English is hard to learn because it doesn't *look* like it sounds and it doesn't *sound* like it looks. Yes, that is very true because there are only twenty-six letters in the English alphabet but there are about forty-six different sounds. This means that a single letter may have many different sounds. One example (perhaps the most famous) is the sound of /sh/. There are thirteen different spellings for that sound: *sh*oe, *s*ugar, is*s*ue, man*s*ion, mis*s*ion, na*t*ion, suspi*c*ion, ocean, conscious, chaperon, schist, fuchsia, pshaw. Should that keep you from learning English? No! Just listen and read and soon those sounds will come naturally. The more you listen and read, the faster you will learn English.

A very famous English writer, George Bernard Shaw, once asked his friends to pronounce the word *ghoti*. Of course, it was a word he made up as a joke. He pronounced it as *fish*, combining the *gh* sound in enou*gh*, the *o* sound in w*o*men, and the *ti* sound in na*ti*on. Yes, English does not sound like it looks.

But, on the positive side, think about the grammar. When you are learning nouns in English, you don't have to worry about the gender of nouns. When native English speakers learn French, Spanish, Portuguese, Italian, German, Russian, Arabic, Hebrew, Greek, or the Slavic languages, to name only a few, they have to learn the gender of each and every noun! They have to worry if *the table* or *the pen* or *the vegetable* is masculine or feminine (or neuter). In languages such as Thai, Japanese, or Hopi, for example, English speakers have to learn certain words for *I, thank you,* etc., depending on their own gender. Not having to learn gender reduces the amount of memorization, social tension, and learning by an enormous amount. See, you *are* lucky to be learning English!

The word *you* can also pose problems. When Americans study Korean, Vietnamese, Armenian, French, Spanish, Portuguese, Italian, German, Russian, Arabic, Cantonese, Thai, Mandarin, or Japanese, for instance, they have to learn all the various ways of addressing the "second" person. There are so many different ways of saying *you*, and if the wrong word is used, the speaker is considered extremely impolite and can get into terrible social trouble. But as an ESL student, you don't have to worry. Whether you are talking to your mother-in-law or your teacher, the president of the United States or your best friend, the one you love or the one you hate, one person or a group of people, someone who is younger than you or someone who is older, someone who is richer or someone who is poorer, a woman or a man, your employee or your employer, a police officer or a stranger on the bus—it's always the same—when it comes to the second person *you* is the one and only word to use, and it is always polite and correct. Oh, you are so lucky to be learning such an easy and safe language as English!

When Americans have to learn almost any other language in the world, they have to worry about grammar rules *all the time*. The nouns have to agree with the adjectives and the articles. You don't have to worry about that at all in English, do you? I can buy the *large, red* apple or ten *large, red* apples and the *large* stays *large, red* stays *red,* and *the* stays *the*. I just add an *s* to most nouns when referring to more than one. And just think about the verbs! In most other languages, using verbs correctly can be a nightmare! The English-speaking person learning a second language has to think *all the time* about which pronoun to use (and there are so many more pronouns in other languages than the few in English) and then match the correct verb ending with the correct form of pronoun. Just think how easy it is for you in English. For example, you need to learn the verb *walk* and then you can say, I *walk* and you *walk* and they *walk* and we *walk*. You have to remember just one little detail: Add an *s* for the *he, she,* or *it.* And if you need to change the time—the tense—then it's all the same: I and you and she and he and it and we and they all *walked.* I and you and she and he and it and we and they all *will walk.* "Oh, but the irregular verbs," you say. But you need to just memorize them once—and they come in patterns. You don't have to worry about each and every ending every time you talk or listen or read or write. Oh, you are so lucky to be learning such an uncomplicated language as English!

So why is English so confusing to you when it should be so easy? Why doesn't it look like it sounds. Why are there so many exceptions to the grammar and spelling rules? Why does it have the largest vocabulary in the world? The main reason is because, unlike most other languages, English is not just one language but a mixture of many very different languages.

More than two thousand years ago there was a group of people living in what is now England. They were called the Celts, and they spoke their own language, Celtic. They were invaded in 55 B.C. by Julius Caesar, who called the island Britannia. The Romans stayed about 450 years, and then the island was invaded by many different tribes of people who lived in what is now northwestern Germany. Those tribes spoke many different languages, but all the languages belonged to the same branch of Indo-European languages: Germanic. One of those tribes was called the Angles and one was called the Saxons. About 1,500 years ago, for various reasons (war, lack of food, adventure, etc.) and at many different times, the Angles and the Saxons traveled across the water to the island of Britain. They fought the Celts and won. They also fought each other. But very slowly, after A.D. 460, the two languages and cultures, Angle and Saxon, were becoming one language and one group of people: the Anglo-Saxons. They created a written alphabet of symbols and lived in England (Angle-land) for over 700 years. They were often invaded by tribes from Scandinavia, whose languages also had a Germanic base. Each time, words were added to the Anglo-Saxon language.

In 1066, King William of Normandy (France) invaded England, fought the Anglo-Saxon king Harold, and won the war. William then ruled England, and French became the official language of England for 300 years. However, French didn't replace the Anglo-Saxon language; it simply added new vocabulary words (over 10,000 words!). For example, the animals of the field cared for by the

Anglo-Saxon farmers were called *calf, cow, pig, chicken,* and *sheep.* The animals were then cooked by the French chefs, who called the meat *veal, beef, pork, poultry,* and *mutton.* In English, words continue to be added to the language, but they aren't subtracted. That is one reason why English has the most vocabulary words of any language (600,000 words plus 500,000 more scientific and technical words). Here are a few examples from everyday English of Anglo-Saxon words with French synonyms. The first word is the Anglo-Saxon; the word in parentheses is from the French: answer (respond), begin (commence), freedom (liberty), sight (vision), snake (serpent), ask (demand), cupboard (cabinet), love (affection).

By the 1400s a true English language was formed. It was a spoken language with a strong written literature, a grammar that came from its Germanic roots, and a large French vocabulary. During the Age of Science in the 1500s an enormous number of Greek and Latin words that describe science and philosophy were added to English. In the Age of Exploration when England fought with Spain and began to conquer and colonize India, Asia, Africa, and the New World, new ideas and items needing names were brought to England from all over the world. With these new items came names from the other countries. Here are some "English" words that came from other languages: *banana* and *banjo* from Africa; *tea* and *ketchup* from China; *coach* and *vampire* from Hungary; *traffic* from Italy; *apricot, assassin, cotton,* and *alcohol* from Arabia; *ginger, pal,* and *bungalow* from India; *hamburger* and *frankfurter* from Germany; *tomato* and *chocolate* from Spain through the Aztecs of Mexico; and *robot* from Czechoslovakia.

Usually, each time a new word is added, the spelling of the word is modeled after the spelling and pronunciation of the native language, and that is one of the reasons why English spelling can seem so strange.

Today about 25 percent of all English words, and most of the basic everyday one-syllable words, come from the original Anglo-Saxon: *the, home, enough, dog, work, mother, father, man, wife, though, child, book, walk, do, eat, go, love, drink, fight, red, black, blue, good, bad,* etc. Another 25 percent of English words come from French. About 10 percent come from Greek, 20 percent come from Latin, and the remaining 20 percent come from the rest of the world.

English grammar is basically old German that has been changed, simplified, and modernized over time. Because the grammar rules were written using rules of classical Latin, they often don't fit, which is why there are so many exceptions to the rules.

It may help to think of English as a fast food hamburger: It is made up of many different parts, but put together as one, it is delicious and easy to get fast!

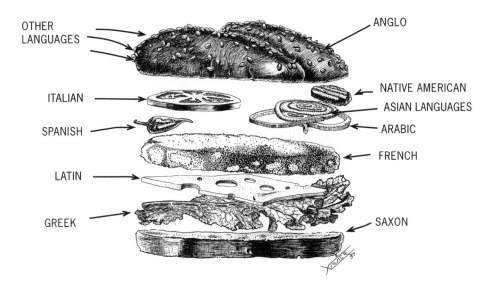

The stories in this book will help you build your own language burger, teach you where the different ingredients came from, and teach you how to put them all together as English. Try it. You'll like it!

Part

Building English and Culture with Fables

A proverb is one man's wit and all men's wisdom.
—Lord John Russell (1792–1878)

Nothing ever becomes real till it is experienced—even a proverb is no proverb to you till your life has illustrated it.

—John Keats (1795–1821)

A Brief History of Aesop, Fables, and Proverbs

Parents from all cultures want to teach the lessons of life to their children so that they can protect them from harm and ready them for the adult world. What better way for children to learn those lessons than from short stories that entertain them and at the same time teach the values of their culture.

A story that teaches an important moral lesson is called a *fable*. Fables have been an important part of many cultures from the very beginning of human civilization. The fable form appeared early in the development of primitive people as part of the oral tradition. It is often a story about animals with human characteristics. The stories were told from parent to child over thousands of years, and this was how cultural values and the language were passed down through generations. The lesson of a fable is usually summed up in one sentence at the end—the *moral*. The moral often becomes a *proverb*—a sentence that states a basic truth about life or gives a general rule of behavior, which is an integral part of the idiom of a language and culture.

The first *written* fables that have been found come from Egypt, 1500 B.C.

The most famous fables in the English language and American culture come from a man named Aesop, who was born a slave in Greece around 620 B.C. As an adult, Aesop was given his freedom because of his intelligence. Aesop traveled through many parts of Greece, teaching and talking with famous philosophers. Through stories he tried to teach lessons that warned about the bad qualities of humans, hoping that people who heard the stories would learn how to improve their behavior.

One day, the very rich king Croesus sent Aesop to give money to the citizens of Delphi. When Aesop saw the people's reaction to the money, he told them that they were too interested in money, and he sent the gold back to Croesus. The people in Delphi became so angry that they killed Aesop by throwing him over a cliff.

You might have read or heard some of Aesop's fables in your own language. Although his stories are well-known, very little is known about him. Many think that he collected stories that were popular at the time, perhaps adding his own. There are well over 300 fables in English that are considered to be written or collected by Aesop.

Aesop's stories have survived because they describe universal human problems and teach simple standards of right and wrong. Stories about talking animals teach lessons about the good and bad qualities of human beings, our virtues and vices. This kind of fable or story always has a moral, a lesson at the end. The stories might describe animals, but the humans who hear the story know who the lesson is really for.

Hundreds of years after the death of Aesop, stories from Asia and ancient times were added to the fables. The stories of Aesop were translated into Latin in A.D. 315 to be used as Latin grammar lessons. A famous Italian teacher, Lorenzo Valla, translated the fables into more modern Latin that were printed using a printing press in 1480. Those Latin fables were immediately translated into English by John Caxton of England and printed in 1485. It has been said that in the Western world, books of Aesop's fables are second only to the Bible in popularity.

The Fox and the Grapes

Reading Readiness

A. With a partner, read this advice column. Describe the situation that is discussed. Try to guess the names of the characters in this story and what the story will be about.

B. Think about these questions and share your ideas with the class.
1. Describe something you desperately want to have.
2. Have you ever wanted something very badly, and then when you couldn't get it, you decided you never wanted it because there was something wrong with it? If so, explain.

Background Notes

This fable is considered to be one of Aesop's most famous. It is about some grapes and a small reddish-brown animal known for its intelligence. This fable gives us a very important idiom in English, "sour grapes." See if you can figure out the meaning of that idiom after reading the fable.

Reading Selection

Now read this story once, as quickly as possible, for the general idea. Try to guess the meanings of the words you don't understand by the context. You can underline the words you don't know, but don't stop reading.

Ask Zenobia

Dear Zenobia,

My older sister never really liked me. I got married first, have two lovely children, and have a great career. She has always struggled for money and lived alone, but now she is finally getting married. I offered to lend her my wedding dress. I know it will save her money that she can otherwise use toward the wedding, and the dress is a perfect fit. She said she always hated it and doesn't need any help from me. She doesn't even want me to be the matron of honor. I'm really hurt. Should I pursue this or just leave it alone?

Little Sis, Wrightsville Beach

Dear Little Sis,

It sounds like sour grapes to me. Since she can't have what you have had, she's criticizing you. Just leave it alone and wait for her to come to you for help. If she doesn't, that's her way of reaching her own independent success. Go to the wedding as a guest and be happy for her.

There was once a fox who saw a beautiful bunch of ripe purple grapes hanging from a vine. The grapes were so fat they looked like they would burst with sweet juice. The fox's mouth watered as he gazed at the grapes.

The vine was trained to grow on the branch of a tall tree, so the fox realized he would have to jump to reach the grapes. The first time he jumped, he missed the grapes. The next time, he first walked back a short distance and then with a run and a jump tried to reach the grapes. He failed. He tried one more jump, but he missed again.

Then he sat down and looked at the grapes in disgust. "What a fool I am trying to get that bunch of grapes. They're probably sour, anyway," said the fox, belittling the grapes. Then he walked away with his nose in the air.

Checking Your Comprehension

After reading this story once, what do you think the answers to these questions are? It's OK to guess, and it's OK to not know the answers yet.

1. Why did the fox want to eat the grapes?
2. How did he try to get them?
3. Why did he decide he didn't want them?

Be a Vocabulary Detective

Working in pairs, look for hints and guess the vocabulary from the context clues. Then fill in the blanks with the correct answers.

Clue 1

This is a story about a *fox* who sees a *bunch* of grapes.

1. A *fox* is _____ (n).
    a) an animal   b) a fruit   c) a tree

2. A *bunch* is _____ (n).
    a) one only   b) a group   c) a fruit

Clue 2

The grapes on the *vines* were so *ripe* and full of their sweet juice that they looked like they would soon *burst*.

3. A *vine* is _____ (n).
    a) something to drink   b) a climbing plant   c) a tall tree

4. *Ripe* means _____ (adj).
    a) ready to eat   b) not ready to eat   c) spoiled

5. To *burst* is _____ (v).
    a) to go up in the air   b) to remain   c) to explode

Clue 3

The fox *gazed* at the grapes. They looked so delicious that they made the fox's *mouth water*. But they were too far away.

6. To *gaze* is _____ (v).
    a) to look away   b) to blink   c) to look at

7. To make the *mouth water* is _____ (idiom/v).
    a) to want to eat   b) to want to swim   c) to spill

Clue 4

The fox *belittled* the grapes because he couldn't have them. He pretended he felt *disgust* for the grapes.

8. To *belittle* is _____ (v).
    a) to like   b) to criticize   c) to be small

9. *Disgust* means _____ (adj).
    a) desire   b) fear   c) intense dislike

Questions for Discussion

First, reread the story carefully, looking for the deeper meanings and reviewing the vocabulary. Then in small groups discuss the following questions with your classmates. Be sure to tell what your native culture is.

1. What was your favorite sentence in this story and why?
2. What do you think the American idiom "it's sour grapes" means?
3. Have you heard this fable in your culture? What was the moral in your culture?

Finding the Moral

In small groups read the following proverbs and decide which of these proverbs best fits the moral of this story. Then share your answer with the class.

a. The grass is always greener on the other side.
b. If at first you don't succeed, try, try again.
c. Beggars can't be choosers.

Now, turn to page 196, find the moral in your list of proverbs, and check it off. Can you think of any other proverbs that will fit the moral?

Double-checking the Vocabulary

Look at the definitions and cross out the words in the list that match. Then, looking at the words that remain, read from left to right, top to bottom, and find the answer to the question, "What did the grapes say to the fox?"

a. to look at for a long time
b. to criticize, to find fault with
c. a small, doglike, meat-eating animal with a long bushy tail
d. to want to eat
e. intense dislike
f. a group of things joined together
g. to explode
h. a type of climbing plant with thin twisting stems
i. ready to eat, mature

We're	fox	bunch	sweet	it's	mouth waters
burst	you	vine	who	ripe	disgust
is	gaze	belittle	sour		

Cultural Notes: Some important values in the United States are to aim high, to not give up without trying hard, and to not settle for less than you want. Of course, one should be realistic and try to achieve one's goals in a practical way. The general belief is that if you want something and are willing to work hard to get it, there is no reason why you shouldn't try to achieve it. An important philosophy is, if you fail, at least you know you tried your best. John Greenleaf Whittier (1807–92), a famous American poet, said

> Of all sad words
> Of tongue or pen,
> The saddest are these:
> "It might have been."

Writing

Think, *in English,* about these cultural values and then, in correct American form and as briefly as possible, discuss the similarities or differences of these values with values in your culture.

Speaking

Share your ideas about these values with the class.

The Hare and the Tortoise

Reading Readiness

A. With a partner, look at this advertisement. Describe what you see. Try to guess the names of the characters in the story and what the story will be about.

If the hare had used *Second* **Wind, the story would have had a different ending.**

Second **Wind Caffeine Booster: the picker-upper when you're falling behind on the job.**

B. Think about these questions and share your ideas with the class.
1. Which lesson do you think your mother would have felt was more important for you to learn: (a) you must never be proud or (b) take your time and do it right?
2. Does a rabbit or a turtle have any special symbolism in your culture? If so, describe it.

Background Notes

Here is another of the more famous of Aesop's fables. This is the story of a hare and a tortoise who have a race. You know who will win, don't you?

Reading Selection

Now read this story once, as quickly as possible, for the general idea. Try to guess the meanings of the words you don't understand by the context. You can underline the words you don't know, but don't stop reading.

There was once a hare who made fun of a tortoise because he was too slow. "You will never get anywhere," the hare laughed.

"I can get where I'm going sooner than you think," said the tortoise, and with that he challenged the hare to a race.

The hare thought this was a great joke. The race began, and the hare was soon far ahead. Knowing he would win, he lay down to take a little nap while he waited for the tortoise to catch up.

Meanwhile, the tortoise kept going slowly and steadily. After a while, he passed the hare, who was now snoring in the shade. When the hare woke up, he saw the tortoise crossing the finish line. He ran as fast as he could, but he could not win the race.

Checking Your Comprehension

After reading this story once, what do you think the answers to these questions are? It's OK to guess, and it's OK to not know the answers yet.

1. Why did the hare laugh at the tortoise?
2. Why did the tortoise challenge the hare?
3. Why did the hare lose the race?
4. Why did the tortoise win the race?

Be a Vocabulary Detective

Working in pairs, look for hints and guess the vocabulary from the context clues. Then fill in the blanks with the correct answers.

Clue 1

This is a story about two animals: a *hare* who thinks he is fast and a *tortoise* who may be slow but who doesn't give up.

1. A *hare* is _____ (n).
   a) a rabbit   b) a horse   c) something on a head

2. A *tortoise* is _____ (n).
   a) a snail   b) a turtle   c) a snake

Clue 2

The tortoise *challenged* the hare to a race. The hare knew he could win the race, but something happened, and try as he might, the hare couldn't *catch up.*

3. To *challenge* means _____ (v).
   a) to dare   b) to lose   c) to agree

4. To *catch up* means _____ (v).
   a) to fall behind   b) to reach   c) to go ahead

Clue 3

The hare thought he had plenty of time, so he took a *nap* in the *shade,* and he immediately began to *snore.*

5. A *nap* is _____ (n).
   a) a short sleep   b) a noise   c) a snack

6. *Shade* is _____ (n).
   a) the sun   b) the grass   c) a shadow

7. To *snore* is _____ (v).
   a) to make a sound   b) to yawn   c) to dream

Clue 4

The tortoise was slow but *steady.* Sometimes those who are very fast don't win.

8. To be *steady* is to be _____ (adj).
   a) hesitant   b) forgetful   c) consistent

Questions for Discussion

First, reread the story carefully, looking for the deeper meanings and reviewing the vocabulary. Then in small groups discuss the following questions with your classmates. Be sure to tell what your native culture is.

1. What was your favorite sentence in this story and why?
2. Which animal did you identify with and why?
3. Discuss the symbolism of animals in your culture; for example, does a pig, snail, bird, frog, dragon, butterfly, spider, etc., have special meaning? If so, what?

Finding the Moral

In small groups read the following proverbs and decide which of these proverbs best fits the moral of this story. Then share your answer with the class.

a. Slow and steady wins the race.
b. Haste makes waste.
c. Better late than never.

Now, turn to page 196, find the moral in your list of proverbs, and check it off. Can you think of any other proverbs that will fit the moral?

Double-checking the Vocabulary

Fill in the crossword with the following vocabulary words: hare, tortoise, challenge, to catch up, nap, snore, shade, steady.

Across

3. unchanging
7. to come up from behind and be equal
8. to make noise while sleeping

Down

1. a small, quick animal with long ears, an upper lip divided in two parts, a short tail, and long back legs that enable it to run fast
2. a shelter from direct sunlight
4. a small, moving, land animal covered by a hard shell into which the legs, tail, and head can be pulled for protection
5. to demand that someone compete
6. to sleep for a short time, especially during the day

Cultural Notes: "Time" is very valuable in the United States. In fact, Americans tend to think of time the same way they think of money. Time is extremely precious. Americans say that time *is* money. They *spend* time and *spend* money. Americans tend to not like to *waste* time or *waste* money. In America, be sure to be exactly on time to a dinner party, to a class, to a test, to a wedding, and especially to a job interview! In fact, in most languages, when you talk about *attention,* you "put" it, but in English you "pay" attention. Don't forget, time is money, and it should never be thrown away.

Writing

Think, *in English,* about these cultural values and then, in correct American form and as briefly as possible, discuss the similarities or differences of these values with values in your culture.

Speaking

Share your ideas about these values with the class.

The Goose and the Golden Egg

Reading Readiness

A. With a partner, look at this advertisement. Describe what you see. Try to guess the names of the characters in the story and what the story will be about.

Golden Goose Reel Estate Investment Audiotapes

Learn how to make wise investments on income property. We guarantee that you will receive dependable monthly income each and every month.

24 Kt.

You can't kill this goose—it keeps giving and giving.
1-777-NEST-EGG

B. Think about these questions and share your ideas with the class.
   1. Which do you prefer, having something wonderful all at once or enjoying small parts of it over a long period of time?
   2. Do you think that greedy people should be punished? Why? Why not?

Background Notes

If you remember how Aesop died, you might wonder if he had forgotten the lesson of this famous fable of his. Do you remember that when Aesop decided to not give the gold to the greedy people of Delphi, they became so angry that they threw him over a cliff. Perhaps if Aesop had remembered what happened to the goose that laid the golden eggs, he would have followed the instructions of King Croesus, delivered the gold to the people of Delphi, and lived to write more fables. Read the story and decide.

Reading Selection

Now read this story once, as quickly as possible, for the general idea. Try to guess the meanings of the words you don't understand by the context. You can underline the words you don't know, but don't stop reading.

There were once a farmer and his wife who possessed the most wonderful goose anyone could imagine. Every day when they went to her nest, the goose had laid a beautiful, shiny egg made entirely of gold.

They would take the eggs to the market and sell them, and soon the farmer and his wife became very rich and famous. But in time, the more money they had, the greedier they became. When the farmer went to visit the goose each morning, he became more and more impatient that there was only one golden egg waiting for him.

One day the farmer couldn't wait any longer. He thought that if he cut the goose open, he could get all the eggs at once. So that is just what he did. But to his sad surprise, when he looked inside, there was not a single egg, and now his wonderful goose was dead!

Checking Your Comprehension

After reading this story once, what do you think the answers to these questions are? It's OK to guess, and it's OK to not know the answers yet.

1. What is special about the goose?
2. What does the farmer think will happen if he cuts the goose open?
3. What actually does happen when the farmer cuts the goose open?

Be a Vocabulary Detective

Working in pairs, look for hints and guess the vocabulary from the context clues. Then fill in the blanks with the correct answers.

Clue 1

The farmer and his wife *possess* a very special *goose*. Every day they find a *shiny* egg of pure gold in the goose's *nest*.

1. To *possess* means _____ (v).
    a) to eat   b) to own   c) to sell

2. A *goose* is _____ (n).
    a) a large ducklike bird   b) a talking bird   c) a bird that hides its head in the sand

3. *Shiny* is _____ (adj).
    a) bright   b) dull   c) delicious

4. A *nest* is _____ (n).
    a) uncombed hair   b) a box   c) a bed made by an animal

Clue 2

The farmer and his wife are very *greedy*. They want all the eggs at once and become very *impatient*.

5. *Greedy* is _____ (adj).
    a) wanting everything   b) generous   c) tired

6. To be *impatient* means to be _____ (adj).
    a) a sick person   b) unable to wait   c) calm

Questions for Discussion

First, reread the story carefully, looking for the deeper meanings and reviewing the vocabulary. Then in small groups discuss the following questions with your classmates. Be sure to tell what your native culture is.

1. What was your favorite sentence in this story and why?
2. If the farmer and his wife had asked you for advice, what would you have told them?
3. Do you think they deserved the punishment they got?

Finding the Moral

In small groups read the following proverbs and decide which of these proverbs best fits the moral of this story. Then share your answer with the class.

a. Nothing ventured, nothing gained.
b. A bird in the hand is worth two in the bush.
c. Don't burn your bridges until they are crossed.

Now, turn to page 196, find the moral in your list of proverbs, and check it off. Can you think of any other proverbs that will fit the moral?

Double-checking the Vocabulary

Fill in the crossword with the following vocabulary words: goose, nest, impatient, shiny, greedy, possess.

Across

1. extremely bright
3. a large bird with webbed feet, a long neck, and a mean disposition
4. to own something
5. a small bed made by an animal, of wood, fur, or paper, usually for its babies

Down

2. unable to wait
3. wanting everything

Cultural Notes: "Don't kill the goose that lays the golden egg" and a similar proverb, "don't bite the hand that feeds you," are common expressions you may hear or read in everyday situations in the United States. As you already know, proverbs stay in a language to teach important cultural lessons. Perhaps these proverbs are common in America to serve as a warning of the dangers of taking for granted what we already have; a warning to not be impatient when we can't find the easiest and fastest way. It is said that Americans too often take their freedoms, the riches of their land, and their democracy for granted. You might have heard of the low numbers of voters in current elections, the low percentage of those concerned about the environment. Americans are often warned that if their democratic form of government and their land is not now maintained and cared for, it will be lost for the future generations. Many predict that the American values of hard work, patience, and planning for the future are being replaced by selfish desires to have an easy life and to have it all now.

Writing

Think, *in English* about those statements and then, in correct American form and as briefly as possible, discuss the similarities or differences of these values with values in your culture.

Speaking

Share your ideas about these values with the class.

The Ants and the Grasshopper

Reading Readiness

A. With a partner, look at this advertisement. Describe what you see. Try to guess the names of the characters in the story and what the story will be about.

B. Think about these questions and share your ideas with the class.
1. What do you think is more important, living for the present or preparing for the future?
2. What might happen if you spend more time playing than working?

Background Notes

This Aesop's fable about ants, small quiet insects famous for working hard as a group, and a grasshopper, a large green insect with large back legs used for jumping and for "singing," teaches a universal lesson about the value of hard work. But to Americans who live on farms, the word grasshopper reminds them more of a serious danger. These insects have been on the earth for over 300 million years and are very, very hungry. Sometimes, there are so many of them, they eat every plant in sight, causing people and animals to die from starvation. If you come from a country which has very little rainfall, you will understand the danger of too many grasshoppers. Their cousin, the cricket, is smaller and brown. At night, the male sings love songs to his girlfriend by rubbing his legs together. Perhaps love has taken away his appetite, for crickets are not dangerous to farmers like grasshoppers are. Maybe you caught a cricket when you were little and kept it in a little cage. The green grasshopper means bad luck to farmers, but in some countries, the brown cricket means good luck to all. Read this fable and decide what kind of luck the grasshopper has.

Reading Selection

Now read this story once, as quickly as possible, for the general idea. Try to guess the meanings of the words you don't understand by the context. You can underline the words you don't know, but don't stop reading.

One bright sunny day at the end of autumn, some ants were scurrying around and drying out some of their store of grain that had gotten damp in the rain. A starving grasshopper came over and humbly asked for some food. All he had was a fiddle in his hand.

"But why are you so hungry?" the ants asked. "Didn't you store away food during the summer?"

"Well, to tell the truth," whined the grasshopper, "I didn't have the time. I was so busy making music on my fiddle that the summer was gone before I realized it."

"Well, if you spent the summer singing, then you will have to spend the winter dancing," said the ants. They shrugged their shoulders in disgust, turned their backs on the grasshopper, and returned to their work.

Checking Your Comprehension

After reading this story once, what do you think the answers to these questions are? It's OK to guess, and it's OK to not know the answers yet.

1. What are the ants doing with the grain?
2. Why is the grasshopper hungry?
3. Why won't the ants help the grasshopper?
4. How do the ants feel about the grasshopper?

Be a Vocabulary Detective

Working in pairs, look for hints and guess the vocabulary from the context clues. Then fill in the blanks with the correct answers.

Clue 1

The ants are *scurrying* around working very hard. They don't have a lot of time to dry the *damp* grain in the sun before the wet and cold winter comes.

1. To *scurry* is _____ (v).
   a) to take your time   b) to hurry   c) to eat

2. *Damp* means _____ (adj).
   a) dry   b) great quantity   c) slightly wet

Clue 2

The grasshopper is *starving* because he played music on his *fiddle* all summer instead of working. He is a little embarrassed to ask for food so he asks *humbly*, but he is a complainer and he *whines* to the ants.

3. To be *starving* is _____ (v).
   a) to need water   b) to need food   c) to need money

4. A *fiddle* is _____ (n).
   a) a musical instrument   b) a game   c) a tape recorder

5. To be *humble* means to be_____ (adj).
   a) conceited   b) unhappy   c) acting lower than others

6. To *whine* means _____ (v).
   a) to make a drink from grapes   b) to cry   c) to make an unpleasant noise or complaint

Clue 3

The ants feel *disgust* for the grasshopper. They don't respect or feel sorry for him. It's not their problem if the grasshopper is hungry, so they just *shrug* their shoulders.

7. *Disgust* is _____ (n).
   a) a feeling of respect   b) a feeling of distaste   c) a feeling of hunger

8. To *shrug* means _____ (v).
   a) to frown   b) to raise the eyebrows   c) to raise the shoulders

Questions for Discussion

First, reread the story carefully, looking for the deeper meanings and reviewing the vocabulary. Then in small groups discuss the following questions with your classmates. Be sure to tell what your native culture is.

1. What was your favorite sentence in this story and why?
2. Do you think the ants should have helped the grasshopper?
3. Does the grasshopper deserve the punishment he will receive? (He might starve to death.)

Finding the Moral

In small groups read the following proverbs and decide which of these proverbs best fits the moral of this story. Then share your answer with the class.

a. There's a time for work and a time for play.
b. Make hay while the sun shines.
c. All work and no play makes Jack a dull boy.

Now, turn to page 196, find the moral in your list of proverbs, and check it off. Can you think of any other proverbs that will fit the moral?

Double-checking the Vocabulary

Look at the definitions and cross out the words in the list that match. Then looking at the words that remain, read from left to right, top to bottom, and find the answer to the question, "What did the ants tell the grasshopper?"

a. a type of violin
b. slightly wet

c. to be extremely hungry
d. intense dislike
e. to raise one's shoulders as an expression of doubt or lack of interest
f. to move fast, with short quick steps
g. acting as if you are in a lower position than another
h. to make a high, sad, complaining sound

disgust	scurry	you'll	damp	just
starve	have to	humbly	shrug	fiddle
eat	whine	your	words	

Cultural Notes: In 1620 the Puritans came from England to establish a colony in America where they could live a life based on their religion. They believed that working hard was the way to Heaven, and that wasting time was the road to Hell. This emphasis on the importance of hard work and its rewards for the future is no longer a religious ideal in America, but it is still a basic value of American culture. In fact some Americans have been called "workaholics" and often suffer from stress-related diseases caused by over-work. The Puritans worked hard to get into Heaven, modern Americans work hard so they will have a comfortable future, whether it's planning for a family or for retirement, to someday own their own home, to travel, etc. Often, on the birth of a baby, the parents will open a savings account to pay for the child's college tuition, eighteen years in the future. And just as the Puritans saw danger in wasting time, so modern Americans distrust "doing nothing" and believe they should always be doing something. Even when Americans go to the beach, have picnics, or relax at home, they often try to plan some sort of activity, take something to read, or a game to play. Doing nothing in public is called loitering and it is against the law!

Writing

Think, *in English*, about these cultural values and then, in correct American form and as briefly as possible, discuss the similarities or differences of these values with values in your culture.

Speaking

Share your ideas about these values with the class.

The Fox and the Crow

Reading Readiness

A.   With a partner, look at this advice column. Describe the situation that is discussed. Try to guess the names of the characters in the story and what the story will be about.

B.   Think about these questions and share your ideas with the class.

1.   Do you believe that people who compliment you are telling the truth, or do you think they want something from you?

2.   In your culture, what do you say when someone gives you a compliment? For example, if someone says, "What a nice looking suit," "What a pretty sweater," etc., what is the polite response?

Background Notes

This fable by Aesop was retold in French by Jean de La Fontaine (1621–95). La Fontaine was greatly admired by another French writer, Voltaire who said, "In most of his fables, he is far superior to those who wrote before and after him, whatever language they may have written in." This particular fable ("Le Renard et la Corneille") has to be memorized, in French, by countless American high school students who take French in school. Aren't you lucky you just need to read this in English?

Ask Zenobia

Dear Zenobia,

My mother is seventy-five years old and recently widowed. My father left her very wealthy. She says she has fallen in love with her hairdresser, who is forty years old. He tells her she is the most beautiful woman in the world and his dream wife. He wants to marry her. I tell her he is just after her money, but she is sure that he is telling the truth. He is very clever and has charmed her so that she won't listen to me or my sister. By the way, she is not very beautiful and looks more than her age! Do you think it's our right to interfere?

Upset, New York

Dear Upset,

Yes, I think you do have a right to interfere. He obviously is using flattery to get your mother to marry him. If she does, the rest of her life could be a nightmare. You could suggest that she put all her savings in a trust for her children. If he truly loves her and marries her, then you and she will know that it wasn't for what she had, but for who she is.

Reading Selection

Now read this story once, as quickly as possible, for the general idea. Try to guess the meanings of the words you don't understand by the context. You can underline the words you don't know, but don't stop reading.

Once there was a crow sitting high up on the branch of a tree. She had a very large and delicious piece of cheese in her beak. A hungry fox came by and smelled the cheese. Looking up at the crow, the clever fox said, "Oh, madam, you are so noble. Your plumage is exquisite. If your voice could match your beauty you would indeed be the queen of birds." The crow was extremely flattered by these compliments and wanted to show the fox that she could sing. She opened her beak and gave a loud "caw." As she did this, out dropped the cheese, and the fox, of course, snatched it. "You have a voice, madam, but it is too bad you do not have wits. You should never trust a flatterer."

Checking Your Comprehension

After reading this story once, what do you think the answers to these questions are? It's OK to guess, and it's OK to not know the answers yet.

1. Why does the fox flatter the crow?
2. Why does the crow lose the cheese?
3. Is the fox telling the truth?

Be a Vocabulary Detective

Working in pairs, look for hints and guess the vocabulary from the context clues. Then fill in the blanks with the correct answers.

Clue 1

The fox *flatters* the crow when he gives her a *compliment* and tells her that her *plumage* is *exquisite*.

1. To *flatter* means _____ (v).
   a) to say something nice   b) to insult   c) to beg

2. A *compliment* is _____ (n).

    a) a rude comment   b) a polite comment   c) an angry comment

3. *Plumage* is _____ (n).

    a) a dress   b) feathers   c) fur

4. *Exquisite* means _____ (adj).

    a) ugly   b) beautiful   c) expensive

Clue 2

When the crow *caws,* she opens her *beak,* and out comes the *delicious* cheese, which the fox immediately *snatches.*

5. To *caw* means _____ (v).

    a) to make a harsh sound   b) to bark like a dog   c) to sing

6. A *beak* is _____ (n).

    a) teeth   b) lips   c) a hard mouth

7. *Delicious* is _____ (adj).

    a) soft   b) expensive   c) good tasting

8. To *snatch* means _____ (v).

    a) to grab   b) to eat   c) to throw away

Clue 3

The fox tells the crow she doesn't have any *wits.*

9. *Wits* means _____ (n).

    a) beauty   b) intelligence   c) a lovely voice

Questions for Discussion

First, reread the story carefully, looking for the deeper meanings and reviewing the vocabulary. Then in small groups discuss the following questions with your classmates. Be sure to tell what your native culture is.

1. What was your favorite sentence in this story and why?
2. Do you think the fox deserved the cheese?

3. Has anyone ever tricked you the way the fox tricked the crow? Or, have you ever tricked someone in this way?

Finding the Moral

In small groups read the following proverbs and decide which of these proverbs best fits the moral of this story. Then share your answer with the class.

a. You can't have your cake and eat it too.
b. Don't bite off more than you can chew.
c. A fool and his money are soon parted.

Now, turn to page 196, find the moral in your list of proverbs, and check it off. Can you think of any other proverbs that will fit the moral?

Double-checking the Vocabulary

Look at the definitions and cross out the words in the list that match. Then, looking at the words that remain, read from left to right, top to bottom, and find the answer to the question, "What did the photographer fox say to the crow?"

a. feathers
b. to grab suddenly
c. the hard mouth of a bird
d. extremely beautiful
e. to say nice things, usually insincerely, generally to receive something in return
f. intelligence
g. the harsh sound of some birds, such as seagulls or crows
h. tasting very good
i. to express praise or admiration

flatter	smile	beak	and	plumage
caw	say	compliment	exquisite	delicious
cheese	snatch	wits		

Cultural Notes: In the United States, Americans generally accept a compliment with a smile and a simple "thank you." For example, when an American says, "Oh, your coat is so nice! Oh, I love your jacket. It looks great on you!" the person being complimented looks the other person in the eye, smiles, and says, "Thank you." In many cultures the opposite is true, and it is polite to instead say "Oh, this is not nice! Oh, this is old! Oh! This old rag?!" In other cultures, the article will be offered as a gift to the person who makes the compliment: "Here, take it, it is yours." In all cultures, the person is saying thank you, but in different ways.

The differences in tradition come from the superstitions of long ago. Our ancestors felt that there was an invisible evil in the world who looked for someone to hurt. It was called the *evil eye*. They believed that if evil heard something good—for example, "Oh! Your baby is so beautiful! Oh, you are so lucky! Oh, what a nice coat"—that the evil spirit would come and take the good luck away and replace it with bad luck: A bad accident might happen to make the baby ugly, the coat would get torn, etc. So to fool the evil eye, our ancestors would say loudly, "Oh! This is not really nice at all." This action became part of the language tradition of most cultures. However, America is a new country and has few of the Old World superstitions as part of its traditions. So, in the United States, when someone tells you that your English is really good, smile, look the person in the eye, and just say, "Thank you!" (Remember to put your tongue between your teeth and blow out air when you say the *th* of *thank*!)

Writing

Think, *in English,* about these responses to compliments and then, in correct American form and as briefly as possible, discuss the similarities or differences of these responses with the appropriate reply to compliments in your culture.

Speaking

Share your ideas about these responses to compliments with the class.

The Little Boy Who Cried Wolf

Reading Readiness

A. With a partner, look at the headline and read the article. What phrase is repeated? Do you think they are really talking about a wolf? Try to guess the names of the characters in the story and what the story will be about.

B. Think about these questions and share your ideas with the class.

1. In your culture, what is the definition of a "lie"?

2. In your culture what is the punishment for a "lie"?

Background Notes

This is possibly Aesop's most famous fable and it is found all over the world. The moral is simple: Do not tell a lie. However, there are two different endings, depending on the culture. Pay particular attention to the ending and compare it with the story in your country. Share your ideas with the class.

TRAGEDY STRIKES: BOY CRIES WOLF

LOS ANGELES—Thirteen-year-old Jim Goldstone placed four false 911 calls Wednesday morning "just messing around," he said. Then Wednesday afternoon his grandmother, seventy-year-old Aleta Potter, collapsed on the kitchen floor. Jim ran to the phone and dialed 911 in earnest, but the operator saw the record of the false calls and didn't believe him. By the time Jim got his neighbor to make the call, it was too late. Paramedics arriving on the scene pronounced Aleta Potter dead, and a very shaken teenager has vowed to never cry wolf again.

Reading Selection

Now read this story once, as quickly as possible, for the general idea. Try to guess the meanings of the words you don't understand by the context. You can underline the words you don't know, but don't stop reading.

Once upon a time there was a little boy whose father was a shepherd. The father and son worked together guarding the sheep of their village. One day the father said to the little boy, "I have to go to town. You must guard the sheep by yourself. If a wolf comes, cry, 'Wolf, wolf!' and the men of the village will come to protect you."

That night the little boy wondered what would happen if he cried, "Wolf, wolf!" So he did. All the men of the village came running as fast as they could to protect the little boy and the sheep. But there was no wolf. The men were very angry. The next night the little boy cried, "Wolf, wolf!" again. Once more all the men of the village came running as fast as they could to protect the little boy and the sheep. But, again, there was no wolf. The men were furious.

The next night there was a full moon. The little boy heard a strange noise, and all the sheep became frightened. He saw an enormous wolf. It had big, red eyes, and its large sharp teeth shone in the moonlight. It looked very, very hungry. Of course the little boy was extremely frightened. He cried, "Wolf, wolf!" as loudly as he could, but nobody came. He cried, "Wolf, wolf!" again, but the men did not believe him. Then the hungry wolf ate the little boy.

Checking Your Comprehension

After reading this story once, what do you think the answers to these questions are? It's OK to guess, and it's OK to not know the answers yet.

1. What happened to the little boy? Did that surprise you?
2. Why did he cry, "Wolf!" when the wolf wasn't there?
3. Why didn't the men save him?

Be a Vocabulary Detective

Working in pairs, look for hints and guess the vocabulary from the context clues. Then fill in the blanks with the correct answers.

Clue 1

The father was a *shepherd,* and he wanted his son to *guard* the sheep.

1. A *shepherd* is _____ (n).
   a) a farmer   b) a butcher   c) a caretaker of sheep

2.   To *guard* means _____ (v).
     a) to eat   b) to take care of   c) to hurt

Clue 2

Like all children, the little boy was curious, and he *wondered* what would happen
if he cried, "Wolf!"

3.   To *wonder* means _____ (v).
     a) to question   b) to know   c) to travel

Clue 3

The father and son lived in a small *village*. One day the father had to go to
town.

4.   A *village* is _____ (n).
     a) a farm   b) a bar   c) a group of houses

5.   A *town* is _____ (n).
     a) a small city   b) a large city   c) a bad place

Clue 4

The little boy woke the men up twice with false alarms, and the men were
furious.

6.   To be *furious* means to be _____ (adj).
     a) very hungry   b) very angry   c) very frightened

Questions for Discussion

First, reread the story carefully, looking for the deeper meanings and reviewing
the vocabulary. Then in small groups discuss the following questions with your
classmates. Be sure to tell what your native culture is.

1.   What was your favorite sentence in this story and why?
2.   Do you think it makes a difference in the lesson if the boy dies or if the
     sheep get eaten? Explain.
3.   What would be the worst punishment in a group-centered culture—to die or
     to live in shame? And what would be the worst punishment in an individual-
     centered culture—to die or to live in shame?

Finding the Moral

In small groups read the following proverbs and decide which of these proverbs best fits the moral of this story. Then share your answer with the class.

a. Honesty's the best policy.
b. Truth is stranger than fiction.
c. Never lie to your minister, doctor, or lawyer.

Now, turn to page 196, find the moral in your list of proverbs, and check it off. Can you think of any other proverbs that will fit the moral?

Double-checking the Vocabulary

Look at the definitions and cross out the words in the list that match. Then, looking at the words that remain, read from left to right, top to bottom, and find the answer to the question, "What did the wolf think about the little boy?"

a. to protect from harm
b. to not be sure, to be curious
c. extremely angry
d. someone who takes care of sheep
e. a very small city
f. a place with only a few houses

shepherd	he	guard	wonder	furious
was	village	town	delicious	

Cultural Notes: In the United States, it is generally thought that it is OK to make mistakes, but it is never OK to deny that you made a mistake. Americans are taught that it is human to make mistakes and that we all learn from those mistakes, so we forgive mistakes. But, we aren't always willing to forgive a liar. Two of the presidents Americans admire are George Washington and Abraham Lincoln; they were both famous for never lying. In contrast, many Americans remember President Richard Nixon as the only president forced to resign, because he had lied to the American people. Maybe you have heard of the Watergate Scandal. In 1972, while President Nixon was hoping to be re-elected, there was a break-in at the Democratic National Headquarters at the Watergate Hotel in Washington, DC. The burglars were caught attempting to put listening devices in the telephones so that the Republican Party could find out the plans of the Democratic Party. Nixon denied that he had any knowledge of this plan. It was later proven that he had, in fact, authorized the break-in. We will never know if the American people would have forgiven Nixon if he had immediately **told** the truth and apologized for his mistake. History can only state that **he was** not forgiven for lying and left the presidency in disgrace in August, 1974. However, by the time of his death in 1994, the public was also able **to recog**nize the contributions he made while serving the United States as **a senator,** vice president, and president.

Writing

Think, *in English,* about these cultural values and then, in correct American form and as briefly as possible, discuss the similarities or differences of these values with values in your culture.

Speaking

Share your ideas about these values with the class.

Part  2

Building English and Culture with Greek and Roman Myths

> *For mythology is the handmaid of literature; and literature is one of the best allies of virtue and promoters of happiness. . . . Without a knowledge of mythology much of the elegant literature of our own language cannot be understood or appreciated.*
>
> —Thomas Bulfinch (1855)

> *Myth is the secret opening . . . religions, philosophies, art, the social forms of primitive and historic man, discoveries in science and technology, the very dreams that blister sleep, boil up from the basic, magic ring of myth.*
>
> —Joseph Campbell (1949)

Greek and Roman Mythology in Brief

All cultures have myths: stories that help explain the mysteries of the world. Most myths contain religious or magical ideas that are believed when the myth is first created. If you are not a part of the religion or culture that created a particular myth, that myth is seen as an interesting story, a fantasy. If you are a part of that culture or religion, it is not a myth but a belief. *This is very important to understand: One person's myth could be another person's religion.*

The myths you will be reading in this section are stories in which the ancient Greeks and Romans attempted to explain a natural or a historic event. More than three thousand years ago, the early Greeks began developing their religion. It was *polytheistic*, which means that the Greeks believed in many, many gods and goddesses. Each god (or *deity*) had a certain personality and a mixture of very human and magical qualities. The ancient Greek religion grew in strength, and after Greece was conquered by Rome in 31 B.C., many of the myths and stories were adopted by the Romans, who often just changed the names of the gods and heroes from Greek to Latin words.

To the Greeks and Romans, the stories of the gods were their religion. They built many temples to their gods and celebrated many religious holidays in their honor.

In time, the power of Rome weakened. When the Roman emperor, Constantine, converted to Christianity in A.D. 312 the great Roman Empire and its religion began to disappear. But the stories of their gods, the myths, remained. If you have ever been in a museum of Western art, you will have seen many beautiful paintings and sculptures about these stories.

Many of the most famous stories were first told in Greece by poets and in plays. The most famous poet who wrote in Greek was named Homer. He lived around the eighth or ninth century B.C. Later, many of those stories were retold in Latin by a Roman poet named Virgil (70–19 B.C.), and later still by a Roman poet named Ovid (43 B.C.–A.D. 18). When Christianity came to England, around 600 A.D., the Catholic monks read and wrote in Latin, and over time, they translated the works of Homer, Virgil, Ovid, and others into English. Many of the myths were first retold in English in the literature of Geoffrey Chaucer (1343–1400) and in the plays of William Shakespeare (1564–1616).

Why are these stories important to you, an ESL student? You have seen that these stories have been an important part of the English language, literature, art, and music for well over six hundred years. It is easy, then, to understand what an important place these well-known myths have in the literature, vocabulary, idioms, and culture of the English-speaking world. If you want to be fluent in English, you should become familiar with as many of these myths as possible. And they are entertaining, as well!

The following readings will introduce you to some of the most famous Greek and Roman myths known to Americans. These stories will teach you a lot about English vocabulary and idioms, and you will discover the origins of many of our words and proverbs. The stories will also provide a context for a discussion about some of the cultural values of the Western world.

To better prepare you to read these stories, you need to know the "cast of characters." The ancient Greeks believed that before the world was formed there was just complete confusion, which they called Chaos. They thought of Chaos as one of their gods. From Chaos came Mother Earth. Mother Earth had many children, who were giants called Titans. Two of Mother Earth's children ruled the Earth—Chronus and his sister Rhea, whom he married. (They did that a lot in Greek mythology!) They had six children, but Chronus was a terrible father and ate his children. Rhea cooked a dinner that made Chronus sick, and the children came back (never mind the details!); the youngest son, Zeus, killed Chronus and then became the king of the gods.

Zeus and his brothers and sisters lived on Mount Olympus, ate a food called *ambrosia,* and drank a liquid called *nectar.* Because they were gods on Mount Olympus, they could never die (they were immortal), but they had a lot of adventures with humans, or mortals. The myths tell the stories of the adventures of the gods (the immortals) and the humans (the mortals).

To help make these stories and the vocabulary words easier for you to understand and remember, be sure to look carefully at the following list of the names of the major gods and goddesses. Their Roman names are in parentheses. You might want to "dog-ear" (fold down the top corner of the page), or mark, the page so you can easily refer back to it as you read the stories.

The Family of the Gods: Brothers and Sisters
(The Roman name for each one is in parentheses.)

Zeus (Jupiter/Jove)	King of the gods
Hera (Juno)	Wife (and sister!) of Zeus
Demeter (Ceres)	Goddess of Corn, or of growing things
Hades (Pluto)	God of the underworld/Hell
Poseidon (Neptune)	God of the seas
Hestia (Vesta)	Goddess of the home
Athena (Minerva)*	Goddess of wisdom
Aphrodite (Venus)+	Goddess of love and beauty

The Immortal Children of Zeus

Hephaestus (Vulcan)	The blacksmith of the gods, the husband of Aphrodite (Venus)
Ares (Mars)	The god of war and the boyfriend of Aphrodite (Venus)
Apollo	The god of the sun, light, truth, and music
Artemis (Diana)	Goddess of the moon and the hunt, twin sister to Apollo
Hermes (Mercury)	The messenger of the gods/seen with wings on his feet
Dionysus (Bacchus)	The god of wine

Child of Other Gods

Eros (Cupid)	God of love and son of Aphrodite (Venus)

THE GODS OF GREECE

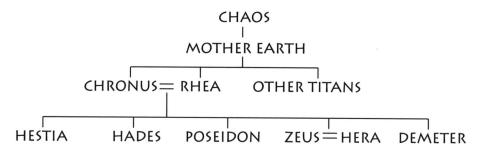

* Athena is the daughter of Zeus. One day he had a bad, bad headache, and she jumped out of his head!

+ Aphrodite also had a strange birth. She is said to be born "of the sea foam"—she rose out of the sea one day. She is generally considered to be related to Zeus.

In the word searches, find the names of the Greek and Roman gods or goddesses in the grids. The names could be written across, backward, or diagonally. See how the examples work.

Greek Gods and Goddesses

M	I	Z	B	U	W	A	E	U	S	C	J	J	R	A
L	D	S	E	Q	P	R	N	U	F	E	S	U	G	R
W	S	F	I	U	O	E	T	I	D	O	R	H	P	A
Y	Y	S	I	M	S	S	H	I	D	Q	Z	Q	I	T
S	S	Z	B	E	E	H	L	O	S	X	E	U	E	E
R	E	B	M	A	I	T	L	O	G	M	M	D	I	U
I	F	R	H	C	D	L	R	O	K	J	L	D	C	L
O	E	P	E	U	O	E	M	A	U	G	R	E	H	K
H	E	D	R	P	N	B	M	N	S	M	T	W	O	A
H	T	W	A	G	V	F	M	E	U	C	C	N	Q	Q
C	K	Q	B	V	Y	E	D	H	T	G	X	G	V	X
P	H	Q	Z	S	F	A	I	T	S	E	H	J	J	Q
E	C	G	O	E	H	A	G	A	Q	W	R	X	F	O

Aphrodite
Apollo
Ares
Artemis
Athena
Demeter
Eros
Hades
Hephaestus
Hera
Hermes
Hestia
Poseidon
✓ Zeus

Roman Gods and Goddesses

✓ APOLLO
CERES
CUPID
DIANA
JUNO
JUPITER
MARS
MERCURY
MINERVA
NEPTUNE
PLUTO
VENUS
VESTA
VULCAN

R	J	R	A	O	A	N	A	I	D	A	Y	S	Y	E
E	N	U	T	P	E	N	V	H	T	F	U	R	O	L
T	W	U	L	F	A	G	R	S	O	N	U	J	M	F
I	L	T	W	C	P	S	E	R	E	C	U	P	I	D
P	G	A	L	F	O	V	N	V	R	G	L	I	N	R
U	O	U	W	K	L	O	I	E	T	P	M	S	Y	U
J	V	O	J	D	L	T	M	A	R	S	X	N	Q	J
J	J	L	G	B	O	R	E	F	U	B	M	T	O	I

Mythology and Legends Word List

In the Appendix at the back of the book, you'll find a place to list the new words you are learning (see p. 207). You will be surprised at how often you will find these words in other books, stories, newspapers, television, movies, cartoons, advertisements, etc. When you have finished reading *Eureka!* you will have learned at least 80 new words and idioms that come from myths.

Let's get started.

1. Look again at the family tree and the names of the gods and goddesses in the "Greek and Roman Mythology in Brief" section and see if you can name three planets named after the Greek and Roman gods and goddesses.

    a. _____

    b. _____

    c. _____

2. This one is more difficult. Think about the terrible story about Chronus eating his children. Do you know the following words?
   chronicle (n): a record of historical events
   chronology (n): the arrangement of events according to their order in time
   chronic (adj): a disease lasting a long time
   d. Can you figure out what they have in common?

    _____

    e. Can you figure out the symbolism of what Chronus meant to the

    Greeks? _____

Be sure to turn to page 207 and add these words to your mythology and legends word list.

Additional Vocabulary Words from Mythology

Have you ever thought about where the names for the days of the week and the months of the year come from? They come from mythology, and they are very old words.

c. Time devours all things.
d. time
a–c. Neptune, Pluto, Venus

The names for the seven days of the week come mostly from the old Anglo-Saxon language but also from the time when the Romans lived in England. In most ancient cultures, people believed that each day should be dedicated to a special god or goddess who would protect them from evil on that day.

Sunday and *Monday* were named for the gods of the sun and the moon.
Tuesday comes from the Anglo-Saxon god of war: Tiw. (It was Tiw's day.)
Wednesday was named for Woden, the king of the gods. (It was Woden's day.)
Thursday was for Thor, the god of thunder. (It was Thor's day.)
Some people think *Friday* was named for Frige, Woden's wife, and some
   think it is for Freyja, the goddess of love. You choose which one you prefer!
Saturday was dedicated to the Roman god of agriculture, Saturn.

The names of the months of the year began in a similar way, but they are all from the ancient Latin language.

In 153 B.C., the Romans changed their calendar. Before that time, their year started in March, which will explain why, if you know Latin, September, October, November, and December don't make mathematical sense. In Latin, *septem* means seven, *octo*, eight, *nouem*, nine, and *decem*, ten. Those months were originally the seventh, eighth, ninth, and tenth months of the year. Later, when the calendar changed so as to begin in January and the month of February was added (September, the seventh month, became the ninth month, etc. *January* was in honor of Janus, the Roman god who had two faces—the god of beginnings and endings; *February* was dedicated to Februaria, the goddess of fertility. *March* was named after Mars, the god of war. *April* is from the Greek Aphro, or Aphrodite, the goddess of love. *May* is for Maia, a goddess of the earth and crops. *June* is for Juno, the goddess of women and marriage (and when do many marriages in the U.S. still occur?). July was named for Julius Caesar and August for Augustus Caesar.

And now you know some secrets that most Americans don't know.

Note: Those of you who speak French, Italian, Portuguese, or Spanish (Latin languages) might be interested in knowing that the days of the week in your languages follow a similar pattern. The Romans named their days of the week after the gods of the sun, moon, Mars, Mercury, Jove, Venus, and Saturn. Figure it out and share with classmates who may not speak your language.

Be sure to turn to page 207 and add these words to your mythology and legends word list.

The Nine Muses

The Greeks believed that Zeus and the goddess of Memory *(Mnemosyne)* /knee-mo-seen/ had nine daughters called *Muses.* Each daughter had a special talent in the arts, and they sang and danced at celebrations on Mount Olympus. Those who worshiped the Muses were very involved in education and study, so it isn't too difficult to guess where the word *museum* comes from, is it?

In Roman times, each Muse was given a more specific talent. It is not necessary for you to remember any of the following names except *Calliope* and *Urania.* Most Americans don't know the specific names either, but they do often hear poets, writers, and artists talk about having a muse or needing their muse to inspire them.

> *Calliope:* Muse of epic (serious, very long) poetry (and the mother of
>   Orpheus)
> *Clio:* Muse of history
> *Euterpe:* Muse of music
> *Erato:* Muse of poetry
> *Terpsichore:* Muse of dance
> *Melpomene:* Muse of tragedy
> *Thalia:* Muse of comedy
> *Polyhymnia:* Muse of singing
> *Urania:* Muse of astronomy

Here are some more details and words to add to your mythology and legends word list.

The goddess of memory, Mnemosyne, has given us many words about memory, like *memory!* There are also *remember* and *memorandum* and its short version, *memo.*

A great way to learn things is to play a trick or game with your memory—to use a *mnemonic.* A popular American students' mnemonic for remembering the names of the Great Lakes is to just remember the word **HOMES.** That mnemonic then helps you remember the names of Lakes Huron, Ontario, Michigan, Erie, and Superior. Think of some mnemonics you use for learning English and share them with the class.

> *Muse:* The Muses used their brains to show their fantastic talents in art and
>   music. No wonder that the words *museum,* to *muse, amuse,* and *amusement*
>   come from them.
> *Urania:* A planet is named after the muse of astronomy: Uranus.

Now, be sure to turn to page 207 and add these words to your mythology and legends word list.

Map of Ancient Greece

Here is a map of what Greece looked like over three thousand years ago. Looking at this map will help you understand the stories. You might want to mark this page so that you can turn back to it while you read the stories.

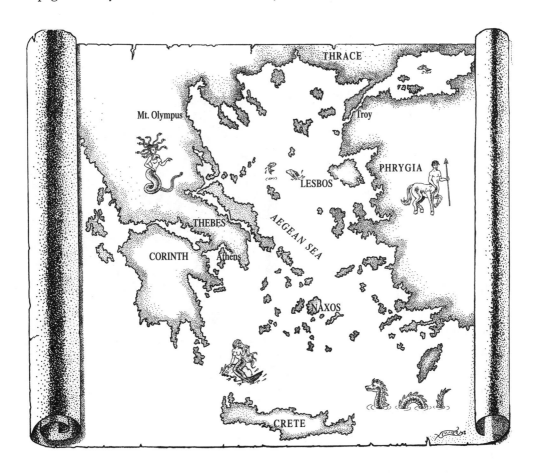

Pandora's Box

Reading Readiness

A. With a partner, look at this political cartoon. Describe what you see. Try to guess the names of the characters in the story and what the story will be about.

B. Think about these questions and share your ideas with the class.

1. Have you ever wondered why there are both good and evil in the world? How do you explain this?

2. What happens when you disobey someone stronger and wiser than you?

Background Notes

This is a "creation myth." It explained to the ancient Greeks and Romans how the world was made. Mostly, it helped them understand the nature of humankind, why there is good and evil in the world, and why humans suffer. It will show you a lot about the polytheistic religion of the Greeks and introduce some of the deities they believed in.

The New Pandora

But there's still Hope!

Cast of Characters

Chaos (kay-ahss): the god of the beginning

Zeus (zoo-ss) (Greek name for Jupiter): king of the gods

Prometheus (pro-me-thee-us): one of the Titans, an uncle of Zeus

Pandora (pan-door-ah): a mortal woman whose name means "the gift of all"

Aphrodite (a-fro-die-tee) (Greek name for Venus): goddess of love and beauty

Apollo (uh-pol-o): the god of light, truth, and music

Hermes (herm-ease) (Greek name for Mercury): the messenger of the gods

Reading Selection

Now read this story once, as quickly as possible, for the general idea. Try to guess the meanings of the words you don't understand by the context. You can underline the words you don't know, but don't stop reading.

A long time ago, before the earth, sea, and heaven were formed, there was only a confused shapeless mass called Chaos. At last, Chaos had two children, Night and Death. There were no light, no sound, and no time. But Night laid an egg into the darkness of Death, and out of that egg came Love, who created Light and Day. And then, from Love and Light came Mother Earth. Mother Earth had many children; they were giants and were called the Titans. The Titans formed the mountains, the rivers, the valleys, and all the animals.

One of the Titans was named Prometheus, and one day the gods instructed him to take some of the earth, mix it with water, and make a man in the image of the gods. Rather than creating a man like the animals that look down to the ground, Prometheus made man stand upright so he could look up at the stars. Without the permission of the gods, however, Prometheus went up to the heavens and brought some fire down from the sun. He gave this to man. With this gift of fire, man was superior to all the animals.

Zeus, the king of the gods, was so angry that he decided to make woman as a punishment for man. The woman Zeus created was named Pandora. All the gods gave her gifts: Aphrodite, the goddess of love, gave her beauty; Apollo, the god of music, gave her singing and dancing; Hermes, the messenger of the gods, gave her the ability to converse and to persuade others; and Zeus, an angry Zeus, gave Pandora a magic box to take with her to earth.

Then Zeus gave Pandora to the brother of Prometheus as a gift. Prometheus warned his brother to beware of gifts that come from the gods; and he told his brother to lock up the box that came with Pandora. Although Prometheus's brother didn't listen, he did tell Pandora to never open the box. One day, however, Pandora was consumed by an incredible curiosity to know what was in that box. She only meant to take a little look. Slowly, she opened the box, but, alas, out rushed all the evil things that the Titans had tried to keep from man: epidemics and diseases, famine, war, jealousy, envy, spite, revenge, and death. Pandora closed the lid as quickly as she could, but all the evil had escaped into the world. There was only one thing left at the bottom of the box, and that was hope.

And so, that is why to this day, no matter what evils make us miserable, we still have hope.

Checking Your Comprehension

After reading this story once, what do you think the answers to these questions are? It's OK to guess, and it's OK to not know the answers yet.

1. Why does Prometheus give fire to man?
2. Why does Zeus want to punish man?
3. Why does Pandora open the box?
4. What was left in the box?

Be a Vocabulary Detective

Working in pairs, look for hints and guess the vocabulary from the context clues. Then fill in the blanks with the correct answers.

Clue 1

The ancient Greeks believed in many, many gods, so their religion was *polytheistic*. Each *deity* had special human qualities. Aphrodite was the *goddess* of beauty.

1. *Polytheistic* means _____ (adj).
    a) believing in many gods   b) believing in one god   c) believing in no god

2. A *deity* is _____ (n).
    a) a god   b) a human   c) the sun

3. A *goddess* is _____ (n).
    a) an angel   b) a human   c) a female god

Clue 2

The Greeks believed that before the beginning of the earth there was nothing but *Chaos*. The *Titans* helped put the confusion in order.

4. *Chaos* means_____ (n).
    a) disorganization   b) organization   c) time

5. A *Titan* is _____ (n).
   a) one who is small   b) a human   c) a giant

Clue 3

Hermes, famous for his ability to make people agree, gave Pandora the gift to *persuade*. Prometheus didn't trust Zeus, and he warned his brother to *beware* of Pandora. Prometheus was right. Zeus had planned that Pandora would open the box of evils.

6. To *persuade* means _____ (v).
   a) to influence   b) to lie   c) to laugh

7. To *beware* means _____ (v).
   a) to trust   b) to be careful   c) to be ignorant

Clue 4

Pandora's curiosity was so strong it was *incredible*. She was so *consumed* by that curiosity, she couldn't resist opening the box.

8. *Incredible* means _____ (adj).
   a) unbelievable   b) cannot be erased   c) believable

9. *Consumed* means _____ (adj).
   a) unmoved by   b) overcome by   c) uninterested in

Clue 5

The box was filled with evils: *epidemics, spite,* and *revenge.* This myth helped the ancient Greeks understand why humans get sick, hate one another, and have wars.

10. An *epidemic* is _____ (n).
    a) spreading of a disease   b) a tree   c) a boat

11. *Spite* is _____ (n).
    a) love   b) hatred   c) old age

12. *Revenge* is _____ (n).
    a) affection   b) getting even   c) food

Questions for Discussion

First, reread the story carefully, looking for the deeper meanings and reviewing the vocabulary. Then in small groups discuss the following questions with your classmates. Be sure to tell what your native culture is.

1. What was your favorite sentence in this story and why?
2. Did this story remind you of any other story you have heard about the beginning of the world? If so, describe it.
3. Did Pandora deserve the punishment she got?

Finding the Moral/Lesson

In small groups read the following proverbs and decide which of these proverbs best fits the lesson of this myth. Then share your answer with the class.

a. Curiosity killed the cat.
b. Hope springs eternal in the human breast.
c. If you play with fire, you will get burnt.

Now, turn to page 196, find the lesson in your list of proverbs, and check it off. Can you think of any other proverbs that will fit the moral?

Double-checking the Vocabulary

Fill in the crossword with the following vocabulary words: polytheistic, deities, goddess, chaos, Titans, persuade, beware, incredible, consumed, epidemic, spite, revenge.

Across

1. to convince
3. a female god
8. unbelievable
10. gods
11. a warning to be careful

Down

1. believing in many gods
2. a serious illness affecting many, many people
4. a feeling of anger and hatred
5. overtaken by something
6. giants
7. getting even with someone
9. complete confusion

Building Vocabulary from Myths

From this story we get many modern words to describe the human experience. Remember that in the beginning there was only *Chaos*. Then there were the *Titans*. Hermes, called *Mercury* in Latin, is the messenger of the gods because he can travel so quickly. He's often pictured with wings on his feet and hat, and he carries a stick with two twisted snakes and wings. Look at the following words and idioms that are now used in common English. They come from the ideas in the story. See if you can match the words and their definitions. The grammar clues will help. Be sure to turn to page 207 and add these words and idioms to your mythology and legends word list.

1. *Titanic* (n)
2. a titan (n)
3. to open Pandora's box (idiom)
4. mercurial (adj)
5. mercury (n)
6. chaotic (adj)
7. chaos (n)

a. very changeable
b. complete confusion
c. to cause trouble that you can't repair
d. a giant
e. confusing, disorganized
f. an extremely large ship
g. an element, like the liquid in a thermometer

Cultural Notes: This myth is thought to have taught the ancient Greeks to understand their place and to not try to be equal to the gods. It also taught that it is very dangerous to question things and to be curious. However, curiosity is generally considered to be a very positive value in America. Our children are taught to question things and to wonder why. In fact, in social situations, people who don't ask questions are sometimes considered boring and impolite!

In addition, being curious is important for citizens of a democracy, for they must be able to question and think for themselves. So, when Americans hear the story of Pandora, they are likely to see the bright and optimistic side to the story—that as bad as things may seem, there is always hope for a better life.

Writing

Think, *in English,* about these cultural values and then, in correct American form and as briefly as possible, discuss the similarities or differences of these values with values in your culture.

Speaking

Share your ideas about these values with the class.

Echo and Narcissus

Reading Readiness

A. With a partner, look at this advertisement. Describe what you see. Try to
   guess the names of the characters in the story and what the story will be
   about.

B. Think about these questions and share your ideas with the class.
   1. Have you ever stood on the top of a mountain and shouted, "Hello," and
      heard your voice come back, "Hello, hello, hello"? Can you explain why
      that happens?
   2. Have you ever known anyone who cares only about him- or herself? If
      so, describe how this person acts.

Background Notes

This is a myth that attempted to explain the reason for echoes, as well as why some people seem to care only about themselves. It is a story about a young woman, who is like a fairy or a spirit, and a handsome young man. Although this myth was originally Greek, it was first retold in English from the Latin, so the names here will be Latin.

Cast of Characters

Jupiter (joo-puh-tur) (Roman name for Zeus): king of the gods
Juno (joo-no) (Roman name for Hera): wife (and sister) of Jupiter
Echo (eh-ko): a nymph
Narcissus (nar-sis-us): a handsome mortal man

Reading Selection

Now, read this story once, as quickly as possible, for the general idea. Try to guess the meanings of the words you don't understand by the context. You can under-line the words you don't know, but don't stop reading.

Once upon a time in ancient days there was a very lovely nymph named Echo. She had a bad habit of talking a lot, and she always wanted to have the last word. Jupiter, the king of the gods, made her become friends with his wife, Juno. He thought that Echo would talk to Juno so much that Juno wouldn't notice when Jupiter went off with his girlfriends! But Juno soon understood what her husband was doing, and she punished Echo: "Since you always want to have the last word, you shall have it." And from that day forward, poor Echo could only imitate the last words of someone else's sentences.

Echo felt very sad that she could no longer say her own words. One day she met a very handsome young man named Narcissus. Echo didn't know that he had many girlfriends and that when he grew tired of them, he would just ignore them and break their hearts. She fell deeply in love with Nar-cissus. He pretended to love her and then, as was his habit, ignored her. This broke Echo's heart, and in her sadness she stopped eating and slowly disappeared, leaving only her sad voice behind.

Narcissus had behaved this way so often that the gods decided to punish him. One day he was walking by a still pond and saw something moving. He knelt down, looked in the pond, and saw a beautiful face. Of course it was his own reflection, but he did not know that. He fell deeply in love with that face. He thought it was a nymph of the water. He begged the nymph to speak to him and come out of the water, but she only made fun of him, smiling when he smiled and leaving when he left. Because the beautiful nymph of the water would not return his affection, Narcissus became so sad he could neither eat, drink, nor sleep. He could not move from the spot and continued to stare at the reflection and beg the nymph to return his love. He disappeared like a candle that burns slowly in the wind. At last, all that was left of Narcissus was a white mark like the melted end of a candle. A pale white flower grew in that place. It's called the narcissus. This flower is very beautiful. It can usually be found on the banks of ponds looking at its reflection in the water.

Checking Your Comprehension

After reading this story once, what do you think the answers to these questions are? It's OK to guess, and it's OK to not know the answers yet.

1. Why does Echo lose her ability to speak her own words?
2. Why does Echo fall in love with Narcissus?
3. What happens to Echo?
4. What happens to Narcissus?

Be a Vocabulary Detective

Working in pairs, look for hints and guess the vocabulary from the context clues. Then fill in the blanks with the correct answers.

Clue 1

Narcissus could only feel *affection* for himself. He *ignored* others. He always *behaved* in that way. It was his *habit* to find new girlfriends.

1. *Affection* means_____ (n).
   a) love   b) hate   c) disinterest

2. To *ignore* means _____ (v).
   a) to not pay attention   b) to not understand   c) to hurt

3. To *behave* means _____ (v).
   a) to act bad   b) to act good   c) to act

4. A *habit* is _____ (n).
   a) a hobby   b) a custom   c) a uniform

Clue 2

When Narcissus passed by a *still pond*, he saw his *reflection* in the water. He thought he saw a beautiful *nymph* living in the water. He had to *kneel* down to see the nymph. He *knelt* there for a while.

5. *Still* means _____ (adj).
   a) unmoving   b) yet   c) theft

6. A *pond* is _____ (n).
   a) a weight of   b) a mirror   c) a small lake
   measurement

7. A *reflection* is _____ (n).
   a) a plant   b) a wave   c) an image

8. A *nymph* is _____ (n).
   a) a young female   b) a fish   c) a cloud

9. To *kneel/knelt* means _____ (v).
   a) to make bread   b) to swim   c) to bend and rest on the
   knees

Questions for Discussion

First, reread the story carefully, looking for the deeper meanings and reviewing the vocabulary. Then in small groups discuss the following questions with your classmates. Be sure to tell what your native culture is.

1. What was your favorite sentence in this story and why?
2. Did Narcissus deserve the punishment he received?
3. Was Echo responsible for her disappearance?
4. Have you ever met a narcissistic person? Describe that person's characteristics and how you felt about him or her.

Finding the Moral/Lesson

In small groups read the following proverbs and decide which of these proverbs best fits the lesson of this myth. Then share your answer with the class.

a.   You reap what you sow.
b.   Silence is golden.
c.   Actions speak louder than words.

Now, turn to page 196, find the lesson in your list of proverbs, and check it off. Can you think of any other proverbs that will fit the moral?

Double-checking the Vocabulary

Look at the definitions and cross out the words in the list that match. Then, looking at the words that remain, read from left to right, top to bottom, and find the answer to the question, "What did Echo say to Narcissus?"

a.   act
b.   love
c.   pretend not to see
d.   not moving
e.   a custom
f.   an imaginary girl, a spirit
g.   what we see in a mirror
h.   a very small lake
i.   bend one's knees

nymph	you	habit	behave	deserved	your
still	kneel	pond	fate	ignore	ate
affection	ate	ate	reflection		

Building Vocabulary from Myths

From this story we get many modern words to describe self-love and how sounds work. Think about what kind of person Narcissus was. Think about how Echo talked. Look at the following words that are now used in common English. They come from the ideas in the story. See if you can match the words and their definitions. The grammar clues will help. Here are some hints: Narcissus was punished because of his *narcissism*. He was so *narcissistic*. He was turned into a *narcissus*.

Echo disappears until only her voice is left. Be sure to turn to page 207 and add these words to your mythology and legends word list.

1. narcissism (n)   a. a fragrant white flower
2. narcissistic (adj)   b. a vibration of sound
3. narcissus (n)   c. caring for just oneself
4. echo (n/v)   d. a personality disorder of being interested only in oneself

Playing Games with Words

Working with a partner, look at the following sentences. They ask a question, and the "echo" answers the question. See if you can figure it out: Look at question 1 for the clue (remember to listen to the sound and not look at the spelling).

1. What do you say when you fall off the **couch**?
2. What is the sound of the elevator door opening in a building?
3. When you're at a picnic, what could make you want to pull down your pants?
4. If you're locked in an elevator, what is the number one terrifier?

Now see how many you and your partner can make up. Share them with the class.

Cultural Notes: A valued characteristic in the United States is to be responsible for one's own actions. In the United States, freedom is a value that can be traced back to the country's fight for independence and the Declaration of Independence and Constitution. As a result, Americans have learned that they have been given the freedom to choose how to behave, but with this freedom comes the knowledge that if one makes the wrong choice, one must be willing to pay the consequences of that action.

Writing

Think, *in English,* about these cultural values and then, in correct American form and as briefly as possible, discuss the similarities or differences of these values with values in your culture.

Speaking

Share your ideas about these values with the class.

Minerva and Arachne

Reading Readiness

A. With a partner, look at this advertisement. Try to guess the names of the
    characters in the story and what the story will be about.

B. Think about these questions and share your ideas with the class.
    1. Have you ever felt that you could do something better than others and
        told them so to their faces? What happened?
    2. Have you ever watched a spider spin a web? If so, describe how it is
        done.

Background Notes

This myth explains a fact of nature—why spiders spin webs. It is also a story that tried to teach the Greeks that humans should never try to be equal to or better than their gods. It was translated into English from the Latin of the writer Ovid, so the names will be from the Latin.

Cast of Characters

Jupiter (Roman name for Zeus): king of the gods
Minerva (Roman name for Athena): goddess of wisdom
Arachne (uh-rak-nee): a mortal girl

Reading Selection

Now read this story once, as quickly as possible, for the general idea. Try to guess the meanings of the words you don't understand by the context. You can underline the words you don't know, but don't stop reading.

One day, when the earth was new and Jupiter had just become the king of the gods, he had a throbbing headache. Suddenly his head opened, and out leaped his daughter Minerva, fully grown and clothed in armor. She became the goddess of wisdom, as well as the goddess of the useful arts like navigation and needlework and defensive war.

Many years later, Minerva heard of the boast of a mortal girl named Arachne. Arachne was very talented at weaving, spinning, and needlework, and she told her friends that she could beat Minerva at any spinning and weaving contest.

Minerva turned herself into an old woman and went to visit Arachne. "Daughter, I have heard of your boast. Please listen to my advice. Challenge your fellow mortals, but never compete with a goddess. In fact, you would do well to beg the forgiveness of the goddess Minerva, and, as she is merciful, she may pardon you."

But Arachne only became angry and said, "Old woman, keep your ideas to yourself. I am not afraid of the goddess; just let her try to beat me in spinning and weaving." At this the goddess resumed her true form, Minerva, but Arachne was not afraid.

The contest began: Each sat down at a spindle to spin wool into thread and then went to a loom to weave.

Minerva wove a most beautiful cloth of many bright colors, showing the triumphs of her father, uncles, aunts, sisters, and brothers—all the gods and goddesses who lived on Mount Olympus. The cloth looked as if it had been painted with a fine brush.

Arachne spun and wove as fast and as gracefully as Minerva. She chose to show the failings and errors of the gods. She showed many different scenes, such as when Jupiter left his wife, Juno, and came to earth to ravish mortal women.

When Minerva saw the subjects Arachne chose to create, she became indignant at the insult. She ripped Arachne's beautiful cloth to shreds and touched Arachne on the head so that she would feel her shame.

Arachne suddenly realized the error of her ways and could not go on living. She committed suicide by hanging herself from a tree. When Minerva saw this, she felt pity for the poor mortal and touched her, saying, "Live, guilty woman, that you may preserve the memory of this lesson, and may you continue to hang, you and your descendants, forever." At her touch, Arachne's hair fell off, as did her nose, ears, legs, and thumbs. Her body shrank up, her head grew small, and the four fingers she had left on each hand attached to her sides and grew into long thin legs. You may see her even today, spinning still, often hanging suspended by her head in the same position as when Minerva transformed her into an *arachnid*, a spider.

Checking Your Comprehension

After reading this story once, what do you think the answers to these questions are? It's OK to guess, and it's OK to not know the answers yet.

1. Why does Arachne challenge Minerva to a contest?
2. Why does Minerva take the disguise of an old woman and go to visit Arachne?
3. Why does Minerva stop the contest?
4. What happens to Arachne?

Be a Vocabulary Detective

Working in pairs, look for hints and guess the vocabulary from the context clues. Then fill in the blanks with the correct answers.

Clue 1

Jupiter had a *throbbing* headache. Then Minerva sprang out of his head, fully dressed in *armor* (no wonder Jupiter had such a bad headache!).

1. *Throbbing* means _____ (adj).
   a) pounding   b) hungry   c) light

2. *Armor* is _____ (n).
   a) pajamas   b) metal clothes   c) a bathing suit

Clue 2

Minerva is a goddess, and she can never die. She takes care of *navigation* and also watches over the *needlework* of women. Arachne is a *mortal* and can die.

3. *Navigation* is _____ (n).
   a) traveling on the seas   b) flying through the air   c) spinning
   or air

4. *Needlework* is _____ (n).
   a) cooking   b) sewing   c) baby-sitting

5. A *mortal* is _____ (n).
   a) a god   b) a goddess   c) a human

Clue 3

Arachne *boasts* that she is better than Minerva. Minerva weaves a design about the *triumphs* of the gods but Arachne weaves a design about their weaknesses instead of their strengths. She weaves a design about how Jupiter *ravishes* women.

6. To *boast* means _____ (v).
   a) to brag   b) to lie   c) to compliment

7. A *triumph* is _____ (n).
   a) a loss   b) a victory   c) a car

8. To *ravish* means _____ (v).
   a) to take care of   b) to hurt   c) to employ

Clue 4

Minerva tells Arachne that she is often *merciful*, but instead of listening to the goddess, Arachne challenges Minerva. When Minerva sees what Arachne has woven about her family of gods, she becomes *indignant* and tears the cloth to *shreds*.

9. To be *merciful* means to be _____ (adj).
    a) happy   b) forgiving   c) sad

10. To be *indignant* means to be _____ (adj).
    a) full of anger   b) full of fear   c) full of thirst

11. To *shred* is _____ (v).
    a) to cut in small pieces   b) to build a little house   c) to lose hair

Clue 5

Arachne feels such shame that she *commits suicide* by hanging from a tree.

12. To *commit suicide* is _____ (v).
    a) to have a baby   b) to murder   c) to kill oneself

Questions for Discussion

First, reread the story carefully, looking for the deeper meanings and reviewing the vocabulary. Then in small groups discuss the following questions with your classmates. Be sure to tell what your native culture is.

1. What was your favorite sentence in this story and why?
2. Did Arachne deserve the punishment she received?
3. Why did Minerva want Arachne's descendants to continue living as spiders?

Finding the Moral/Lesson

In small groups read the following proverbs and decide which of these proverbs best fits the lesson of this myth. Then share your answer with the class.

a. Pride goes before a fall.
b. A stitch in time saves nine.
c. He who laughs last, laughs best.

Now, turn to page 196, find the moral in your list of proverbs, and check it off. Can you think of any other proverbs that will fit the moral?

Double-checking the Vocabulary

Look at the definitions and cross out the words in the list that match. Then, looking at the words that remain, read from left to right, top to bottom, and find the answer to the question, "What did Arachne get for dinner?"

a. capable of dying, opposite of immortal
b. to tear into pieces
c. to pound strongly and rapidly
d. to kill oneself
e. to seize with violence, to rape
f. to direct the course of a ship or plane
g. strong, protective, metal covering
h. feeling surprised anger at something that should not be
i. artistic sewing done with needle and thread
j. to talk proudly
k. victory
l. willing to forgive instead of to punish

throb	armor	she	navigate	shred	caught
boast	mortal	a	merciful	triumph	needlework
big	ravish	indignant	fat	commit suicide	fly

Building Vocabulary from Myths

Turn to page 207 and add the following word to your mythology and legends word list. *Arachnid* is the scientific name for the family of spiders. Did you ever see the movie *Arachnophobia*? What do you think it is about?

Cultural Notes: In the United States being honest about one's abilities and good qualities, but never conceited, is a valued trait. In a job interview, the interviewer may ask "What are your good points? Why should we hire you?" A very good answer is to smile and look the interviewer in the eyes and say, "I am responsible and reliable. I come early and stay late. I am self-motivated and well qualified, and I will be an asset to your company." (Of course, you can only say this if it is true!) This type of response may be considered rude in some cultures in which the applicants must lower their eyes, bow their heads, and act very humble. Many cultures teach humility—that it is impolite to boast about how good you are. America is different: It's expected that you will state the facts, and if the facts are complimentary, then it's good for you!

Writing

Think, *in English,* about these cultural values and then, in correct American form and as briefly as possible, discuss the similarities or differences of these values with values in your culture.

Speaking

Share your ideas about these values with the class.

King Midas and the Golden Touch

Reading Readiness

A. With a partner, look at this advertisement. Describe what you see. Try to guess the names of the characters in the story and what the story will be about.

The **Midas Touch** can be yours!!!
With our three-hour sales video:

How to Sell Every Customer through the Golden Touch Plan

Learn how to turn all your sales calls into money.
Only $19.95.
Credit card payments, no C.O.Ds
Call 1-777-GET RICH

B. Think about these questions and share your ideas with the class.

1. Have you ever wanted something very much only to get it and then regret it? If so, describe the situation.
2. Is it easy or difficult for you to keep a secret? Explain.

Background Notes

This Greek myth is about two different experiences in the life of a very greedy king, who gets what he wishes for, and his barber, who can't keep a secret. The story is set near the River Pactolus, which is in the country of Turkey. The myth has been retold many times in English literature, especially by the famous English writer Geoffrey Chaucer, who was writing in the late 1300s. Have you ever seen a *Midas Muffler Store*? Guess where this company got its name.

Cast of Characters

King Midas (my-das)
his daughter
Bacchus (baa-kus) (Roman name for Dionysus [die-oh-ni-sis]): the god of the wine
Silenus (suh-lee-nus): the favorite of Bacchus
Pan: the god of the fields
Apollo: the handsome god of music

Reading Selection

Now read this story once, as quickly as possible, for the general idea. Try to guess the meanings of the words you don't understand by the context. You can underline the words you don't know, but don't stop reading.

Once upon a time in ancient Greece, there lived a very greedy king who loved gold very much. The only thing he loved more was his daughter. One day he met Silenus, who was a favorite of Bacchus, the God of the Wine. Silenus was ill and King Midas took him to his palace and cared for him for ten days. On the eleventh day King Midas took old Silenus back to the Temple of Bacchus and Bacchus offered him a reward. "To thank you for your kindness to my beloved friend, I will grant whatever wish you have." "Then I wish that everything I touch will turn to gold," said the greedy king. Bacchus was disappointed with the request, but he granted it nevertheless.

As Midas walked home, he touched the branch of a tree. It turned to gold. Then he picked a flower and it too was transformed into gold. Overjoyed, the king rushed home. His furniture, the plates, the glasses, his clothes all turned to gold when he touched them. But when he called for dinner and picked up a piece of bread, it too turned to gold and he couldn't eat it. He took a sip of wine, but it turned to gold in his throat and he choked. And, alas, when his beloved daughter ran to hug him, at her father's touch, she turned into a statue of gold.

In a panic the king ran to the Temple of Bacchus, begging to be released from this reward that had turned into a curse. "Go to the River Pactolus and plunge your head and body into the water and it will wash away the charm," said Bacchus.

King Midas did as he was told and the charm was removed. If you go to the River Pactolus today, you will know why the sand has been changed to gold.

After this horrible experience, King Midas hated wealth and lived in the countryside and became a worshiper of Pan, the god of the fields.

One day Pan had the audacity to compare his music to the music of the god of music, Apollo. Pan challenged the handsome Apollo to a music contest. King Midas said that Pan was the better musician. Apollo was so angry that he punished Midas for having "stupid ears." Apollo said that the ears of Midas were like the ears of an ass, and at those words from the god, the ears of King Midas grew long and hairy, exactly like the ears of a donkey.

The king was mortified and began to wear a large hat so no one could see his ears and know his shame. But his barber, of course, knew the secret. King Midas threatened the barber with death if he told anyone of the condition of the king's ears. But the barber could not keep the secret. Desperate, the barber went to the banks of a river, dug a very deep hole, and shouted into the hole, "King Midas has asses' ears!" Then he covered up the hole. But before long, a thick bed of reeds grew from that hole and began to whisper the story every time a breeze passed by.

If you go to the banks of a river today and listen carefully to the reeds, you will hear them whisper the secret that King Midas had asses' ears. But maybe you won't understand the words, because the reeds only speak Greek.

Checking Your Comprehension

After reading this story once, what do you think the answers to these questions are? It's OK to guess, and it's OK to not know the answers yet.

1. What does King Midas wish for?
2. Why does he regret his wish?
3. Why does Apollo punish him and how?
4. Why does the barber dig a deep hole?

Be a Vocabulary Detective

Working in pairs, look for hints and guess the vocabulary from the context clues. Then fill in the blanks with the correct answers.

Clue 1

King Midas is very *greedy* and only cares about money and gold. But he finally learns his lesson and decides he doesn't want *wealth*.

1. To be *greedy* means to be _____ (adj).
   a) giving to others   b) wanting everything   c) selling for profit
                               for oneself

2. *Wealth* means _____ (n).
   a) a lot of money   b) a little money   c) loving money

Clue 2

King Midas becomes very frightened when his beloved daughter is *transformed* into a statue of gold. He is *desperate* for help. The king *panics* and runs to the Temple of Bacchus.

3. *Transformed* means _____ (adj).
   a) remaining the same   b) changed   c) moving

4. To be *desperate* means _____ (adj).
   a) having hope   b) losing hope   c) alone

5. To *panic* means _____ (v).
   a) to laugh   b) to cry   c) to fear

Clue 3

Bacchus tells King Midas that he can remove the magic charm if he *plunges* his head and body into the River Pactolus.

6. To *plunge* means _____ (v).
   a) to go down   b) to go up   c) to remain in
                                           one position

Clue 4

Pan has the *audacity* to challenge the god Apollo, and King Midas says Pan is the better musician. Apollo punishes Midas by giving him the ears of an *ass,* and King Midas is *mortified.*

7. *Audacity* is _____ (n).
    a) respect   b) shame   c) disrespect

8. An *ass* is _____ (n).
    a) a horse   b) a donkey   c) an elephant

9. To be *mortified* is to be _____ (adj).
    a) embarrassed   b) dead   c) angry

Clue 5

The barber cannot keep a secret, so he tells the secret to the ground. But the secret turns into seeds that grow into *reeds* that *whisper* the secret whenever the *breeze* blows.

10. *Reeds* are _____ (n).
    a) trees   b) fish   c) grasslike plants

11. To *whisper* means _____ (v).
    a) to talk loudly   b) to not talk   c) to talk softly

12. A *breeze* is _____ (n).
    a) a soft wind   b) a storm   c) a cloud

Questions for Discussion

First, reread the story carefully, looking for the deeper meanings and reviewing the vocabulary. Then in small groups discuss the following questions with your classmates. Be sure to tell what your native culture is.

1. What was your favorite sentence in this story and why?
2. Did King Midas deserve the reward and the punishment he received? Explain.
3. Do you think the barber did the right thing? Could he have done anything different?

Finding the Moral/Lesson

This story of King Midas is really about making choices. In small groups look at the following proverbs and decide which proverb best fits the moral of each part of this story. You may find one proverb for the part about Kind Midas and another proverb about the barber. Then share your answers with the class.

a. All that glitters is not gold.
b. If wishes were horses, beggars would ride.
c. Three can keep a secret, if two of them are dead.

Now, turn to page 196, find the moral or morals in your list of proverbs, and check it off. Can you think of any other proverbs that will fit the moral?

Double-checking the Vocabulary

Look at the definitions and cross out the words in the list that match. Then, looking at the words that remain, read from left to right, top to bottom, and find the answer to the question, "What did King Midas say to his barber?"

a. an animal that looks like a horse with long ears, a donkey
b. to change
c. to be extremely embarrassed
d. to speak very quietly
e. wanting more than one needs
f. a lot of money
g. extreme uncontrollable fear
h. a soft wind
i. the act of dropping down from a height
j. a state of fear because of a loss of hope
k. tall, strong, hollow, grasslike plants that grow in wet places
l. showing no respect

be	greedy	careful	transform	panic	desperate
and	plunge	don't	wealth	audacity	breeze
cut	ass	my	mortified	ears	
too	reeds	whisper	short		

Building Vocabulary from Myths

From this story we get an idiom to describe good luck, a word to describe fear, and an idiom to describe beauty. Remember that the meanings of stories and words often change over time. Look at the following word and idioms that are now used in common English. They come from the ideas in the story. See if you can match the items and their definitions. The grammar clues will help. Be sure to turn to page 207 and add this word and these idioms to your mythology and legends word list.

1. the Midas touch (idiom/n) (very positive idiom in American English)

2. panic (v) (from the god Pan, whose music made people very excited)

3. a perfect Apollo (idiom/n)

a. to be very frightened

b. to have very good luck

c. extremely handsome

Cultural Notes: As already mentioned, this story is really a story about making the right choices. King Midas was offered the choice of anything he wanted and he made the wrong choice. There are many warnings in American culture about what can happen if you make the wrong choice or if you look for the easy way. The old saying "Be careful for what you wish—it might come true" is remembered when Americans watch the classic movie *Gone with the Wind*. In that movie, the handsome Ashley Wilkes warns Scarlet O'Hara, "You are wishing for the moon. What will you do with it, if you get it?" Scarlet makes the wrong choice and has to pay the consequences. King Midas is asked to choose who is the better musician and the barber is given a choice, to keep the secret or to tell it. In the United States, a democratic society where individuals are guaranteed freedom of choice, Americans are taught that if they make the wrong choice, they have no one to blame for their misfortune but themselves. Freedom of choice is not free; one must pay the consequences for their actions.

Writing

Think, *in English,* about this idea of choices and consequences, and then in correct American form and as briefly as possible, discuss the similarities or differences of this attitude with values in your culture.

Speaking

Share your ideas with the class.

Ceres and Proserpine

Reading Readiness

A.   With a partner, look at this advertisement. Describe what you see. Try to guess the names of the characters in the story and what the story will be about.

B.   Think about these questions and share your ideas with the class.
1.   Pretend you are living five thousand years ago and you know nothing about science. How would you explain the seasons of the year? Why is there winter, why is there spring, etc.?
2.   Think about parents' love for their child. How would parents react if their child were kidnapped? How would they feel? What would they do?

Background Notes

This myth was told in a poem in the eighth century B.C. The story became very popular in Rome. The names in this story will be the Latin versions because it came into English from Latin. This myth attempted to explain the changes in the seasons.

Cast of Characters

Jupiter (Roman name for Zeus): king of the gods
Ceres (seer-ease) (Roman name for Demeter): goddess of growing things
Proserpine (pros-er-peen) (Roman name for Persephone [per-sef-uh-nee]):
    daughter of Ceres
Pluto (Roman name for Hades): god of the Underworld
Venus (Roman name for Aphrodite): goddess of love
Cupid (Roman name for Eros): messenger of love

Reading Selection

Now read this story once, as quickly as possible, for the general idea. Try to guess the meanings of the words you don't understand by the context. You can underline the words you don't know, but don't stop reading.

When the world was quite young there was no winter, only spring and summer, and food grew all year round. Jupiter had just become the king of the gods. He sent his sister Ceres to take care of the earth and his brother Pluto to take care of the dead in the Underworld, where Pluto became the king of Hell. One day, Venus, the goddess of love and beauty, sent her son, Cupid, to thrust an arrow of love into the heart of the king of the dead, Pluto.

One fine spring day Pluto left Hell and rode in his black chariot, pulled by four black horses, to earth. Immediately, Cupid shot his arrow, and just as the arrow entered Pluto's heart, he rode past the beautiful young daughter of Ceres, Proserpine, who was gathering flowers with her young friends. Pluto fell instantly in love with Proserpine, grabbed her, and carried her off with him to his palace in the Underworld. Proserpine screamed and struggled, but to no avail.

The young friends of Proserpine ran as fast as they could to tell her mother, Ceres, that Proserpine had been kidnapped. Ceres was so upset that she ceased to care for the earth and agriculture. All the crops died and there was no harvest. Then the animals died from lack of food. Winter covered the earth as Ceres traveled all over the world looking for her beloved child. At long last, weary with searching and forlorn from sadness, she sat on a stone and continued sitting there for nine days. A young child, gathering wood with her father, saw Ceres and said, "Mother, why do you sit on those rocks?" Oh, how sweet that word *mother* was to the ears of Ceres! The father begged her to come to their cottage. "No, thank you," she said, "but be happy with your daughter, for I have lost mine." And as she spoke, tears, or something like tears (for the gods never weep), fell down her face. The father and daughter begged so sincerely for Ceres to come that she finally rose from the stone and followed them to a small, poor hut. Inside was a little boy so sick with a fever that he was near death. The goddess bent over the child and kissed his lips, and he instantly became well. At that moment, Ceres assumed her real form as a goddess and, wrapped in a cloud, flew away to continue her search for her daughter.

A sea nymph came to Ceres and said, "Goddess, blame not the land; it opened unwillingly to yield a passage to your daughter. I have seen her sitting on the throne of the Underworld. She is now the wife of Pluto." Distraught, Ceres immediately flew to Heaven to beg Jupiter for help. Jupiter said that as long as Proserpine had not eaten anything while she was in Hell, she could return to earth. Proserpine was starving and had just eaten six seeds of a pomegranate. The gods decided that, for the sake of the earth, a compromise must be made. For the six seeds Proserpine had eaten, she would stay as Pluto's queen for six months, and the other six months she could remain above the earth with her mother.

So when Proserpine is with her mother, Ceres is joyful and takes care of the earth, and we have spring and summer. But when Proserpine must go to be with her husband, Pluto, Ceres mourns and ceases her work and the earth falls asleep, so we have autumn and winter.

Checking Your Comprehension

After reading this story once, what do you think the answers to these questions are? It's OK to guess, and it's OK to not know the answers yet.

1. Why does Pluto kidnap Proserpine?
2. Why does winter suddenly come to the earth after the kidnapping?
3. Why can't Proserpine return to her mother permanently?
4. According to this myth, why are there four different seasons in the year?

Be a Vocabulary Detective

Working in pairs, look for hints and guess the vocabulary from the context clues. Then fill in the blanks with the correct answers.

Clue 1

Ceres is the goddess of the earth and also the goddess of *agriculture*. When she is happy, plants grow, and there is a good *harvest*.

1. *Agriculture* is _____ (n).
    a) the raising of animals   b) the growing of plants   c) hunting and fishing

2. A *harvest* is _____ (n).
    a) planting plants   b) gathering plants   c) eating plants

Clue 2

Pluto *kidnaps* Proserpine and carries her to the Underworld in a black *chariot* pulled by four black horses. Ceres is extremely *weary* from traveling and searching for Proserpine. She is so *forlorn* with sadness she *ceases* to care about the earth.

3. To *kidnap* means _____ (v).
    a) to steal a person   b) to have a child   c) to go to sleep in
                                                         the day

4. A *chariot* is _____ (n).
    a) something to sit on   b) a carriage   c) divided in equal
                                                         parts

5. To be *weary* means to be _____ (adj).
    a) tired   b) sad   c) angry

6. To feel *forlorn* means to feel _____ (adj).
    a) lonely   b) happy   c) unhappy

7. To *cease* means _____ (v).
    a) to begin   b) to continue   c) to stop

Clue 3

A water *nymph* tells Ceres that her daughter is now queen of Hell, and Ceres is *distraught* when she learns where her daughter is. Her only chance to get Proserpine back is if Proserpine hasn't eaten anything. Alas, Proserpine has eaten six seeds from a *pomegranate*.

8. A *nymph* is _____ (n).
    a) a spirit of the water   b) a fish   c) a plant

9. To be *distraught* means to be _____ (adj).
   a) destroyed   b) extremely upset   c) tired

10. A *pomegranate* is _____ (n).
    a) a steak   b) a fruit   c) bread

Clue 4

Ceres meets a poor farmer and enters his *hut*. The farmer's son is close to death, and, because she saves the boy's life, the family will not have to *mourn*.

11. A *hut* is _____ (n).
    a) a barn   b) a one-room house   c) an apartment

12. To *mourn* means _____ (v).
    a) to feel sadness   b) to pay a bill   c) to wake up
    because of loss

Questions for Discussion

First, reread the story carefully, looking for the deeper meanings and reviewing the vocabulary. Then in small groups discuss the following questions with your classmates. Be sure to tell what your native culture is.

1. What was your favorite sentence in this story and why?
2. What did this story explain to the ancient Greeks and Romans?
3. Do you think that it was fair that Proserpine had to stay six months in the Underworld?

Finding the Moral/Lesson

In small groups read the following proverbs and decide which of these proverbs best fits the lesson of this myth. Then share your answer with the class.

a. The early bird catches the worm.
b. Don't cry over spilt milk.
c. Half a loaf is better than none.

Now, turn to page 196, find the moral in your list of proverbs, and check it off. Can you think of any other proverbs that will fit the moral?

Double-checking the Vocabulary

Fill in the crossword with the following vocabulary words: harvest, agriculture, chariot, kidnap, cease, weary, forlorn, hut, nymph, distraught, pomegranate, mourn.

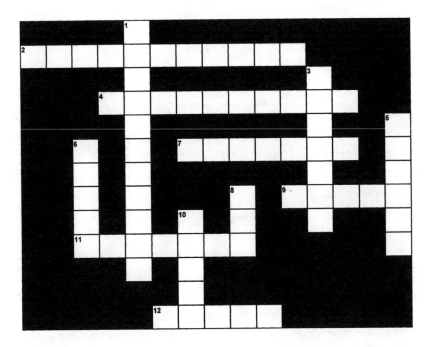

Across

2. a bright red autumn fruit containing many small seeds covered by juicy meat
4. extremely nervous and unhappy, almost to the point of madness
7. left alone and unhappy
9. to feel sadness for the death of someone
11. the time to gather the ripe crops from the fields
12. extremely tired

Down

1. the art or practice of farming and raising crops
3. a two-wheeled horse-drawn seatless vehicle
5. to steal a person
6. a minor goddess of nature
8. a very small shelter usually with only one room
10. to stop

Building Vocabulary from Myths

Look at the following words that are now used in common English. They come from the ideas in the story. See if you can match the words and their definitions. The grammar clues will help. Remember that Ceres is the goddess of agriculture. Be sure to turn to page 207 and add the words to your mythology and legends word list.

1. cereal (n)   a. grains: wheat, rice, corn, etc.
2. cereals (n)   b. breakfast food

Cultural Notes: Being optimistic, instead of pessimistic, is a common attribute of Americans. If something is not perfect, people in the United States try to compromise and make the best of what they have. This value has its roots in the early history of the nation when the lands were vast and everything seemed possible if you worked hard. You may have heard Americans say that life is like a glass of water and hear them say the glass is half *full* not half *empty*. Seeing it half full is optimistic. The famous and beloved Eleanor Roosevelt, wife of President Franklin Delano Roosevelt, worked tirelessly as First Lady and after her husband's death in 1945, she championed the cause of those who were in need. She has often been described by this phrase: "She would rather light a candle than curse the darkness." That quality of looking for the bright side and working for positive results, is generally admired in the United States.

Writing

Think, *in English*, about this cultural value and then, in correct American form and as briefly as possible, discuss the similarities or differences of this value with values in your culture.

Speaking

Share your ideas about this value with the class.

Cupid and Psyche

Reading Readiness

A. With a partner, look at this advertisement. Describe what you see. Try to guess the names of the characters in the story and what the story will be about.

Take aim at your lover's heart. You can't miss with a gift of Cupid chocolates.

Sold at all fine gourmet stores.
Make every day Valentine's Day!

B. Think about these questions and share your ideas with the class.
   1. What makes people fall in love?
   2. What causes love at first sight?
   3. What keeps love alive in a relationship?

Background Notes

Have you ever celebrated Valentine's Day? Can you describe the symbols of that holiday? If you thought of a boy with wings who carries a bow and arrow, you are thinking of Cupid. His story comes from a Greek myth three thousand years ago that tries to explain the strange facts of love. In written mythology, Cupid (his

Greek name was Eros) was the son of Venus (her Greek name was Aphrodite), the goddess of love and beauty. Cupid was the messenger of love, and it was his job to make people fall in or out of love. If he shot someone with a magic arrow tipped with gold, that individual would fall in love with the person he or she saw next. But sometimes Cupid would use an arrow tipped with lead. Ah, then the person would refuse to fall in love. Sometimes Cupid was really mean, and he would shoot one person with a golden arrow, and then, he would shoot the beloved one with a leaden arrow. Has that ever happened to you? This story is about Cupid's falling in love. The names used will be the Roman names because the Latin version from Ovid is the one that was translated into English and is more familiar in America than the original Greek story.

Cast of Characters

Cupid (Roman name for Eros): god of love
Psyche (s-eye-key): a mortal woman
Venus (Roman name for Aphrodite): goddess of love
Ceres (Roman name for Demeter): goddess of growing things
Proserpine (Roman name for Persephone): the daughter of Ceres
Pluto (Roman name for Hades): god of the Underworld
Jupiter (Roman name for Zeus): king of the gods

Reading Selection

Now read this story once, as quickly as possible, for the general idea. Try to guess the meanings of the words you don't understand by the context. You can underline the words you don't know, but don't stop reading.

Once there was a beautiful young princess named Psyche. She was so beautiful that the people said she was even more beautiful than the goddess of love and beauty, Venus. This made Venus so jealous and angry that she called her son Cupid to her and said, "This Psyche must be punished. Somewhere on earth there must be the ugliest, meanest man. I want you to make Psyche fall in love with that man."

That night Cupid filled his quiver (where he kept his arrows) with magic arrows and flew down to earth. He found Psyche asleep in her bed, her left arm thrown across her face. He took a golden pointed arrow from his quiver and touched her shoulder. He was curious about his mother's jealousy, so he gently moved Psyche's arm from her face. He was shocked by her beauty, so shocked that he did not notice that he had scratched himself with the golden point of the arrow. At the same moment Psyche had a dream, and in her dream she saw the handsomest man in the world. As he faded from her dream, she heard him say "Wait for me."

After that dream Psyche refused to see any young men or consider marriage. One summer evening, as Psyche was walking outside dreaming of her "dream man," a friendly wind raised her slowly from the earth and carried her far away to a magnificent palace with beautiful rooms and a lovely table set with delicious food. When night fell, she heard a soft voice saying, "Thank you, Psyche, for waiting." "Who are you?" she asked. "My name you must never know, and my face you must never see. But do not doubt my love. I will be a good husband to you." She believed the voice with all her heart and did not know this was Cupid.

While she was first living with Cupid, Psyche was a very happy and dutiful wife, but in time, she became lonely for her family. She begged Cupid to let her two older sisters come to visit. When they came they turned green with envy because their younger sister was living in a fantastic palace with hundreds of invisible servants and a loving, magical husband. They talked Psyche into doubting her husband. They suggested that he must be a horrible monster and that was why he would only be with her after twilight and he would leave her before dawn. They advised Psyche to hide not only a candle but a large knife under her bed, so she could cut off his head in case he was really a monster. Alas, Psyche listened to her jealous sisters and that night, Cupid came to her as usual just after sunset. Before dawn, Psyche got out of bed and lit a candle. As she bent over to see her husband's face, a drop of hot wax fell from the candle onto Cupid's shoulder. He awoke and looked at her with anger and sadness. "Good-bye, Psyche," he said. "After I left my mother and made you my wife, is this the way you trust me? Love and suspicion cannot live in the same house. So the god of love must go."

Psyche's heart was broken, of course, and she felt guilty that she had betrayed her husband's trust. When she told her sisters the identity of her husband and that he had left her, they were secretly overjoyed. Each one thought that now they could have him as a husband. Without telling the other, they each ran to a high rock and called to the wind to take them to Cupid's palace. They jumped, but the wind wasn't listening, and so they fell to their deaths.

Psyche, meanwhile, wandered sadly around looking for her husband. She saw a temple on a high hill and went inside. She saw a great number of ears of corn mixed with wheat and farming tools on the floor. Being a neat person, she immediately put everything in order. It was the Temple of Ceres (Ceres was the goddess of the earth and the harvest). Ceres, who understood heartbreak because she had lost her only daughter, took pity on Psyche. She advised, "You must go to your mother-in-law, Venus, as horrible as it might be, and beg her for forgiveness." So with her heart pounding and her hands wet, fearing she would be killed, Psyche went to the Temple of Venus. Venus immediately met her with anger. "What a loving wife! My poor son is still in bed because of the wound on his shoulder. You are so ugly and stupid my son could love you again only if you prove you are a neat housekeeper." Then Venus led Psyche to a storehouse filled with an enormous pile of pigeon food: wheat, corn, beans, and rice. "Separate these grains into four piles and put the piles in the four corners of this room before dusk, and I will give you back your husband." Well, what would you have done? You would have fallen on the ground and cried, wouldn't you? And that is just what Psyche did. Luckily, Cupid, who was not as badly wounded as his mother said, heard his beloved wife's cries and sent ants to the storehouse. They immediately went to work and separated the four grains into four neat piles before sunset.

Venus was furious when she saw the job had been done well. The next day she told Psyche to walk across a stream where there were very dangerous sheep with golden wool and to gather as much wool as she could. Just as Psyche stepped into the water she heard the wind tell her to wait until the afternoon when the stream was quiet and the evil sheep were asleep. Then, according to the wind, their wool would be caught on the branches of the bushes. She followed this advice and brought back an armful of golden fleece to Venus. Venus was so angry she told Psyche that she must take a box to Proserpine and ask her to fill it with some of her beauty for "I have lost some of mine because I have had to take care of my sick son." Proserpine was the daughter that Ceres had lost, the one who had been kidnapped by the god of death, Pluto, and now lived as his queen in the Underworld. Psyche was afraid to go to the Underworld and decided to quickly put an end to her misery. She climbed to the top of a high tower, and just as she was about to jump, a voice said, "Why are you such a coward, Psyche? I shall tell you how to find Proserpine." Led by the voice, she found a safe way to the Underworld, met Proserpine, gave her the box and

Venus's message, and soon was on her way back to the earth with the box now filled with beauty. Once in the sunlight, Psyche suddenly felt a great desire to look in the box. "Why can't I take just a little of this beauty and put it on my cheeks? Perhaps my Cupid will love me more." But when she opened the box all that came out was a deep sleep, and she fell to the ground as if she were dead. Cupid came to her, gathered the sleep back into the box, and woke her with a scratch of his arrow. "Oh, Psyche, again you have almost died because of your curiosity! Take this box to my mother, and I will take care of the rest."

Then Cupid flew as fast as he could to his uncle Jupiter—the king of the gods—and begged him to make his beloved Psyche a goddess. Jupiter granted the wish, and the happy couple were soon reunited, this time on Mount Olympus, where the gods all live. In time, they had a daughter, whom they named Pleasure.

Checking Your Comprehension

After reading this story once, what do you think the answers to these questions are? It's OK to guess, and it's OK to not know the answers yet.

1. Why does Cupid fall in love with Psyche?
2. Why does Psyche look at her husband when he told her not to?
3. Name two people who help Psyche.

Be a Vocabulary Detective

Working in pairs, look for hints and guess the vocabulary from the context clues. Then fill in the blanks with the correct answers.

Clue 1

Venus is *jealous* of Psyche, and she feels *envy*. She feels that people will think Psyche is more beautiful, and Venus wants to be considered the most beautiful. Venus wants to *punish* Psyche because she feels competition from her.

1. To be *jealous* is to feel _____ (adj).
   a) sick   b) love   c) anger about what someone else has

2. *Envy* is _____ (n).
    a) hunger   b) jealousy   c) love

3. To *punish* means _____ (v).
    a) to hurt   b) to help   c) to make a joke with
                                                   words

Clue 2

Venus tells Cupid to find the *meanest,* ugliest man in the world—a *monster.* She wants Psyche to fall in love with a horrible man who will treat her very badly.

4. A *mean* person is _____ (adj).
    a) not handsome   b) not fat   c) not kind

5. A *monster* is _____ (n).
    a) extremely horrible   b) extremely kind   c) extremely old

Clue 3

Psyche's sisters make her *doubt* that Cupid is handsome, and she becomes really curious to find out what Cupid looks like. Her *curiosity* causes her to lose Cupid, for he feels that Psyche has *betrayed* him when she looks at him with the candle.

6. To *doubt* means _____ (v).
    a) to question   b) to know   c) to look

7. *Curiosity* means _____ (n).
    a) wanting to leave b) wanting to get   c) wanting to know
                            well

8. To *betray* is _____ (v).
    a) to help   b) to kill   c) to break a promise

Clue 4

Psyche is such a *coward* that she thinks of killing herself. Cupid feels *pity* for his wife, but Psyche doesn't know it, and she can't eat or sleep. She is full of *misery.*

9. A *coward* is _____ (n).
    a) one who is afraid b) one who is   c) one who takes care
                            brave   of cows

10. *Pity* is _____ (n).
    a) happiness   b) love   c) compassion

11. *Misery* is _____ (n).
    a) sadness   b) delight   c) anger

Clue 5

When the candle melts, the hot *wax* falls on Cupid's shoulder. Venus takes care of her son's *wound* from the burn.

12. *Wax* is _____ (n).
    a) a material made   b) a material made   c) a material made
       of meat   of fat   of metal

13. A *wound* is _____ (n).
    a) a sore   b) a shirt   c) hunger

Questions for Discussion

First, reread the story carefully, looking for the deeper meanings and reviewing the vocabulary. Then in small groups discuss the following questions with your classmates. Be sure to tell what your native culture is.

1. What was your favorite sentence in this story and why?
2. Do you think Psyche was right to try to see what her husband looked like?
3. Do you think this story had a moral lesson to it? Discuss your thoughts.

Finding the Moral/Lesson

In small groups read the following proverbs and decide which of these proverbs best fits the lesson of this myth. Then share your answer with the class.

a. Marry in haste, repent at leisure.
b. It was the straw that broke the camel's back.
c. A watched pot never boils.

Now, turn to page 196, find the moral in your list of proverbs, and check it off. Can you think of any other proverbs that will fit the moral?

Double-checking the Vocabulary

Fill in the crossword with the following vocabulary words: to feel jealousy, punished, meanest, monster, curiosity, envy, doubt, betray, pity, wound, misery, coward, wax.

Across

3. a solid material made of fat used for making candles
6. hating someone for having something better than you have
7. a creature that causes fear
10. to feel that you want something someone else has
11. deep sadness
12. to question, to not believe

Down

1. feeling of wanting to know everything
2. compassion
3. a damaged place on the body
4. caused someone to suffer
5. the most unkind, unpleasant
8. to be disloyal or unfaithful
9. one who is very afraid

Building Vocabulary from Myths

From this story we get many modern words to describe love and emotions. Remember that Venus is the goddess of love and beauty. (Her Greek name was Aphrodite.) Cupid is the messenger of love and thus symbolizes love. (*Note:* His

Greek name was Eros.) Psyche symbolizes the mind or soul. Look at the following words that are now used in common English. They come from the ideas in the story. See if you can match the words and their definitions. The grammar clues will help. Be sure to turn to page 207 and add these words to your mythology and legends word list.

1. *cupid*ity (n)
2. *ero*tic (adj)
3. *psych*iatrist (n)
4. *vene*real disease (n)
5. *psych*ologist (n)
6. *Venus* (n)
7. *psych*otic (n)
8. *psych*edelic (n)
9. *aphrod*isiac (n)

a. a medical doctor who treats mental illness
b. sexual
c. a medicine to help sexual abilities
d. the name of a planet in the sky
e. a person with a serious mental disease
f. a drug that alters the mental state
g. a sexual disease
h. a scientist who studies mental functions
i. a very great desire, especially for money or property

Cultural Notes: In the modern United States, equality between the sexes is considered important for many Americans. Equality is an important part of marriage. In a typical modern American marriage, the values are for the husband and wife to share the work, responsibility, decision making, etc. This is due in part to the fact that today many women have careers that are as important to the family's financial stability as the men's. If both are working, both must therefore share in the household chores, child-rearing, etc. It is generally part of the picture for the husband and wife to be equally honest and faithful to each other.

Writing

Think, *in English*, about these cultural values and then, in correct American form and as briefly as possible, discuss the similarities or differences of these values with values in your culture.

Speaking

Share your ideas about these values with the class.

Orpheus and Eurydice

Reading Readiness

A. With a partner, look at this advertisement. Describe what you see. Try to guess the names of the characters in the story and what the story will be about.

Cell phone connections by *Orpheus*

Keep in touch with loved ones 24 hours a day.
Why worry about where your loved ones are?
Give them a call anytime, anywhere.
Out of sight doesn't mean out of mind.

Only $9.95 a month   *Call 1 (777) ORPHEUS*

B. Think about these questions and share your ideas with the class.
1. Would you be willing to sacrifice your life for the one you love? Explain.
2. If you are told not to look at something, can you resist the temptation to look?

Background Notes

This tragic love story from Greek mythology was retold in Latin by the Roman poets Ovid and Virgil. The story is known in English from the Latin translations. Although each retelling changes various details, the basic universal theme of true lovers separated by death has made this story a very popular, constantly retold myth. Two operas have been written about this story, by the Italian composer Claudio Monteverdi and the German composer Christoph Gluck, but, unlike most operas, both composers emphasized a happy ending to this story.

The French poet Jean Cocteau wrote a play about this myth, and it became a famous French movie in 1949. In 1959, the Brazilian movie *Black Orpheus* received many awards and is today considered a classic film. You might want to watch it after you read this story. If you are familiar with the Old Testament biblical story about Lot's wife, you might also find a similarity in one part of this story.

Cast of Characters

Calliope (ka-lie-o-pee): one of the nine muses—the muse of poetry
Orpheus (or-fee-us): the mortal son of Calliope—he plays a stringed instrument called the lyre (liar)
Eurydice (you-rid-i-see): the wife of Orpheus
Proserpine (Roman name for Persephone): daughter of Ceres, queen of the Underworld
Pluto (Roman name for Hades): king of the Underworld
the Maenads (may-i-nads): "crazy" women

Reading Selection

Now read this story once, as quickly as possible, for the general idea. Try to guess the meanings of the words you don't understand by the context. You can underline the words you don't know, but don't stop reading.

Once, in ancient Thrace, there was a child born to the Muse of poetry, Calliope. On his birth, she gave to her son, Orpheus, the gift of poetry and music. Some people even gossiped that Apollo, the god of music, was the real father of Orpheus. No mortal could play as beautifully as Orpheus. When he sang or made music on his lyre, he could quiet wild winds and soothe the savage animals.

When Orpheus was a young man he fell deeply in love with an extremely beautiful young woman, Eurydice, and she fell as deeply in love with him. People said that their two hearts beat as one. On the afternoon of their wedding, as Eurydice and her bridesmaids were gathering flowers in a garden, a former boyfriend tried to kidnap her. As Eurydice ran from him, she stepped on a viper. The snake bit her on her foot, and alas she died. Not even the heavenly music of Orpheus could bring Eurydice back to life, and her spirit was taken, as all spirits, to the Underworld, the kingdom of Pluto, to live as a shadow.

Orpheus's grief was so deep that he threw away all human fear and descended into the Underworld himself to try to find his beloved wife. Because of his magical music, he was able to tame all the monsters that guard the gates to Hell. He knelt before the throne of Pluto and Proserpine and begged to have his wife back. Orpheus said that he knew that all born of woman must come to the Underworld but that Eurydice had come too soon. He said that she was a bud that dropped before the flower could bloom.

Even Pluto, the god of Hell, could not resist the beauty of Orpheus's music and voice, so he decided to give Eurydice back to life but only on one condition: As the two climbed back up to earth, Orpheus must not look back. He must trust the word of Pluto that Eurydice would be following behind. Orpheus agreed, and they climbed up from the darkness toward the light of life. Just as Orpheus stepped into the daylight of earth, he turned. Alas, he turned too soon! His beloved wife was immediately pulled back down to the Underworld, holding out her hands and crying, "Oh, Orpheus, farewell, a final farewell."

Orpheus was inconsolable. He could not eat or sleep. He refused to talk to anyone, especially women, and he spent the days crying and playing his beautiful, sad music. One day, a group of "crazy" women called the Maenads heard him playing. They became furious when he wouldn't talk to them, so they killed the gentle Orpheus, violently tearing him limb from limb and throwing his head into a river. As the head floated it cried, "My darling, Eurydice!" Now Orpheus is with his beloved Eurydice, and together they walk the world of the shadows hand in hand for eternity.

His mother, Calliope, and her Muses gathered and buried the pieces of his body at the foot of Mount Olympus. It is said that birds sing more beautifully there than any other place in the world. Apollo took the lyre of Orpheus and placed it in the sky, where it can be seen in the constellation Lyra.

Checking Your Comprehension

After reading this story once, what do you think the answers to these questions are? It's OK to guess, and it's OK to not know the answers yet.

1. What is the special talent of Orpheus?
2. How does Eurydice die the first time?
3. Why does Eurydice die the second time?
4. How does Orpheus die?

Be a Vocabulary Detective

Working in pairs, look for hints and guess the vocabulary from the context clues. Then fill in the blanks with the correct answers.

Clue 1

Orpheus can make music so beautiful that it *soothes* the *savage* animals and *tames* the winds. People *gossip* that his father might be Apollo, the god of music.

1. To *soothe* means _____ (v).
   a) to make angry   b) to make peaceful   c) to feed

2. *Savage* is _____ (adj).
   a) sweet   b) quiet   c) mean

3. To *tame* means _____ (v).
   a) to anger   b) to calm   c) to kill

4. To *gossip* means _____ (v).
   a) to laugh   b) to talk about someone   c) to give a present

Clue 2

Eurydice is bitten by a *viper*. After her death, Orpheus is *inconsolable* and refuses to say *farewell.*

5. A *viper* is _____ (n).
   a) a crazy woman   b) a poisonous snake   c) a bee

6. *Inconsolable* means _____ (adj).
   a) unable to be comforted   b) accepting   c) not hungry

7. *Farewell* means _____ (n).
   a) hello   b) good-bye   c) a bus ticket

Clue 3

Orpheus describes Eurydice's death as like the dropping of a *bud* before the flower can *bloom*.

8. A *bud* is _____ (n).
   a) a kind of beer   b) a good friend   c) a baby flower

9. To *bloom* means _____ (v).
   a) to develop   b) to die   c) to smile

Clue 4

Orpheus has a horrible death. The Maenads tear him *limb* from limb and throw his lyre away. Apollo places the lyre in the sky in a *constellation*.

10. *Limbs* are _____ (n).
    a) bodies   b) heads   c) arms and legs

11. A *constellation* is _____ (n).
    a) a group of stars   b) an orchestra   c) a planet

Questions for Discussion

First, reread the story carefully, looking for the deeper meanings and reviewing the vocabulary. Then in small groups discuss the following questions with your classmates. Be sure to tell what your native culture is.

1. What was your favorite sentence in this story and why?
2. Do you think Orpheus was justly punished for looking back?
3. Do you think this is a sad story or a happy story?

Finding the Moral/Lesson

In small groups read the following proverbs and decide which of these proverbs best fits the lesson of this myth. Then share your answer with the class.

a. Fool me once, shame on you. Fool me twice, shame on me.
b. Don't count your chickens until they're hatched.
c. Leave well enough alone.

Now, turn to page 196, find the moral in your list of proverbs, and check it off. Can you think of any other proverbs that will fit the moral?

Double-checking the Vocabulary

Fill in the crossword with the following vocabulary words: soothe, savage, tame, gossip, viper, inconsolable, farewell, bud, bloom, limb, constellation.

Across

1. to say things about people behind their backs
4. a leg or an arm
6. to calm, to cause to feel better
8. a group of stars in the sky that make a special pattern or design
10. wild and angry
11. to grow and develop

Down

2. unable to be made to feel better
3. a poisonous snake
5. the beginning of a flower
7. to say a formal good-bye
9. not savage, domesticated

Cultural Notes: Americans tend to accept the fact that human beings make mistakes and feel that if someone makes a mistake once, they should be given another chance. You might notice this concept when you are taking a test. Of course you want to do well the first time, whether it is for your driver's license or for entering college, but if you don't do well, there are always a second and a third and sometimes an unlimited number of chances to try again. The ancient Greeks believed that humans must always obey the wishes of the gods and there was no room for mistakes. Orpheus made one foolish mistake and lost his beloved wife forever. An American might say, "Hey, that was just strike one; he should have had two more chances."

Writing

Think, *in English,* about these cultural values and then, in correct American form and as briefly as possible, discuss the similarities or differences of these values with values in your culture.

Speaking

Share your ideas about these values with the class.

Daedalus and Icarus

Reading Readiness

A. With a partner look at this advertisement. Describe what you see. Try to guess the names of the characters in the story and what the story will be about.

B. Think about these questions and share your ideas with the class.
    1. Have you ever had a dream in which you could fly? If so, describe it.
    2. What usually happens when a child doesn't follow the advice of someone older and wiser?

Background Notes

This is another ancient myth that warned the Greeks to accept their humanity and to never attempt to be as powerful as the gods. It is a very sad story about a father who is a talented builder and his son who doesn't listen to good advice.

Cast of Characters

Apollo (Greek name for Helios): god of the sun, music, and art
King Minos: a powerful king of Crete, a Greek island
Daedalus: a mortal and an architect
Icarus: a mortal and the son of Daedalus

Reading Selection

Now read this story once, as quickly as possible, for the general idea. Try to guess the meanings of the words you don't understand by the context. You can underline the words you don't know, but don't stop reading.

Once upon a time there was a very famous inventor and architect who lived in ancient Greece. His name was Daedalus, and he designed many buildings for a king named Minos. His most famous achievement was to design and build an enormous and intricate maze (labyrinth) in which Minos would put his enemies so that they would never find their way out.

Because Daedalus was the designer, Daedalus knew the secret, and King Minos became afraid that Daedalus would tell someone how to get out of the maze; so he exiled Daedalus to an island from which there was no escape. However, he allowed Daedalus's son, Icarus, to accompany his father in exile. "Minos may control the land and the sea, but not the air," said Daedalus. "I will try to escape that way." Daedalus spent many weeks walking up and down the beach studying the flight of the seabirds.

One day he went to his son and said, "Icarus, go and find all the feathers you can, and I shall make us wings with which to fly to the mainland and escape this exile." "Fly like the gods?" asked the boy. "There are times when men must try to be like the gods," said his father.

The boy did as he was told, and his father took some thread and some wax and made two wings for himself and two wings for his son. They then went to the top of the highest mountain on the island and attached the wings to their arms.

"Icarus, my son, you must be sure to follow the middle way. If you fly too low over the sea, the feathers will become wet and heavy. If you fly too high, the sun will melt the wax."

Then Daedalus jumped from the mountain and soared over the sea with his son following behind. But the boy soon forgot the advice of his father and, overjoyed by his new power, flew high into the sky. The heat of the sun melted the wax, and one by one the feathers fell off. Suddenly when Icarus fluttered his arms, there were no feathers to hold him up so down he plunged and was submerged in the blue sea.

Daedalus saw the feathers floating over the water but could not find his beloved son. When he landed safely on land, he named the place Icaria, and there he built a temple to Apollo, the god of the sun, and hung up his wings as an offering of repentance to the god.

Checking Your Comprehension

After reading this story once, what do you think the answers to these questions are? It's OK to guess, and it's OK to not know the answers yet.

1. Why does Minos exile Daedelus?
2. Where does Minos exile Daedelus?
3. How does Daedelus escape?
4. Why does Icarus die?

Be a Vocabulary Detective

Working in pairs, look for hints and guess the vocabulary from the context clues. Then fill in the blanks with the correct answers.

Clue 1

Daedalus was an *inventor* and *architect*. He could design wonderful things and buildings. He designed a special *maze* (labyrinth), a prison, with turns and rooms, and people got lost inside and could never find their way out. The pattern of the maze was very *intricate*.

1. To *invent* is _____ (v).
   a) to copy   b) to create   c) to enter

2. An *architect* means _____ (n).
   a) a designer   b) a farmer   c) a police officer

3. A *maze* (or labyrinth) means _____ (n).
   a) a garden   b) a surprise   c) a puzzle

4. *Intricate* means _____ (adj).
   a) easy   b) complicated   c) inside

Clue 2

King Minos was afraid Daedalus knew too much, so he *exiled* Daedalus to an island far away from his countrymen.

5. To *exile* is _____ (v).
    a) to send away   b) to invite   c) to breathe in

Clue 3

First Icarus *soared* high in the sky like a bird, with feathers on his arms. But then the wax melted, and Icarus *fluttered* in the air and then fell into the ocean and was *submerged*.

6. To *soar* is _____ (v).
    a) to fall   b) to fly   c) to hurt

7. To *flutter* is _____ (v).
    a) to stay still   b) to say nice things   c) to move quickly

8. To *submerge* is _____ (v).
    a) to go under   b) to go above   c) to stay on the surface

Clue 4

Daedalus realized his mistake of trying to fly like a god and offered his wings to Apollo in *repentance* so that the god would forgive him.

9. *Repentance* means _____ (n).
    a) sorrow   b) happiness   c) anger

Questions for Discussion

First, reread the story carefully, looking for the deeper meanings and reviewing the vocabulary. Then in small groups discuss the following questions with your classmates. Be sure to tell what your native culture is.

1. What was your favorite sentence in this story and why?
2. Did Icarus deserve the punishment he received?
3. Did Daedalus deserve both punishments he received?

Finding the Moral/Lesson

In small groups read the following proverbs and decide which of these proverbs best fits the lesson of this myth. Then share your answer with the class.

a. Look before you leap.
b. Better safe than sorry.
c. Moderation in all things.

Now, turn to page 196, find the moral in your list of proverbs, and check it off. Can you think of any other proverbs that will fit the moral?

Double-checking the Vocabulary

Fill in the crossword with the following vocabulary words: invent, architect, maze, intricate, exile, soar, flutter, submerge, repentance.

Across

1. person who designs and plans buildings
4. containing many detailed parts and difficult to understand
5. to fly far, fast, and high
8. to go under the surface of water
9. to force someone to leave his country

Down

2. sorrow for doing something wrong
3. an arrangement in lines with a central point reached by twists and turns, some of them blocked; a labyrinth
6. to make up or produce for the first time
7. to move quickly and lightly

Building Vocabulary from Myths

From this story we get the word *labyrinth,* which means a very complicated structure of many turns and twists. Maybe you've seen pictures of the inside of the ear. Part of the inner ear is called the labyrinth because it is so complicated in its structure. If it gets infected, the disease is called labyrinthitis and it can make you feel very dizzy. If you feel sick on a boat, car, or a plane, it's caused by the sensitivity of your balance mechanism in your labyrinth. Now, turn to page 207 and add the word labyrinth to your mythology and legends word list.

Cultural Notes: A very important lesson in the ancient Greek religion was that humans should accept their human weaknesses and never try to be equal to the gods. In the United States, however, a very important value is to encourage individuals to try and achieve whatever they desire, even if they might not succeed. American children are taught to never say something is impossible and to reach for the stars. Ralph Waldo Emerson, a famous American writer advised us to "hitch your wagon to a star." There are countless well-known and well-publicized stories of Americans who dared to do the unthinkable; who accomplished what no one thought was possible and who did so because they reached for the stars. Most people who immigrate to America understand that they are taking a great risk, reaching for their dream. They might fail to reach that dream, but then, again, if they don't take a risk, how will they find out if they will succeed?

Look at this part of a poem, loosely translated from a poem by a French poet named Guillaume Apollinaire. It's all about what might happen when you take a risk:

> "Come to the edge" he said.
> "No!"
> "Come to the edge" he said.
> "No, we're afraid."
> "Come to the edge" he said.
> And they did.
> He pushed them off.
> And they flew away like birds.

Writing

Think, *in English*, about this cultural value of taking risks and then, in correct American form and as briefly as possible, discuss the similarities or differences of this value with values in your culture.

Speaking

Share your ideas about this value with the class.

Hercules

Reading Readiness

A. With a partner, look at this advertisement. Describe what you see. Try to guess the names of the characters in the story and what the story will be about.

B. Think about these questions and share your ideas with the class.
1. Briefly describe the characteristics of the most famous hero in your culture.
2. If someone goes insane, do you think that person is responsible for his or her actions and should the individual pay the consequences for those actions?

Background Notes

The story of Hercules is very old. He was the most popular hero of ancient Greece, and there are probably more stories told of his adventures than of any other figure in Greek mythology. He was admired by the Greeks because they thought he was the strongest mortal on the earth. It is possible that the story of Hercules began with stories of the adventures of an ancient prince who lived in Mycenae, Greece. These adventures were part of the ancient Greek oral tradition and changed and became more fantastic with each telling. Most of those stories have been lost, but there are still versions of the stories of Hercules in two tragedies by Sophocles and two by Euripides (famous Greek playwrights), by Pindar (a famous Greek poet), and by other ancient Greeks as well.

The story was later retold in Latin, in Roman times, by the famous poet Ovid. Today you can find many ancient sculptures of Hercules and many famous paintings of the hero in museums around the world. Hercules has also become a comic book hero and a cartoon character. You might want to watch the 1997 Disney movie about Hercules after you read this story and see how much the story has been changed.

Cast of Characters

Since Hercules was the most celebrated hero of Greece, the names in this story are from the Greek, except for the name of Hercules. He was named *Heracles* in Greek (her-uh-kleez) (meaning the glory of Hera), but since the spelling *Hercules* is the most common now in English, that is the name used in this story.

Zeus (Greek name for Jupiter): king of the gods

Hera (Greek name for Juno): wife of Zeus

Hercules: son of Zeus and Alcemena (al-suh-men-uh), a mortal

Megara (me-gar-uh): the first wife of Hercules

Deianira (dee-uh-near-uh): the second wife of Hercules

Atlas: a Titan who holds up the skies

Hades (Greek name for Pluto): king of the Underworld

Hippolyta (hip-o-leet-uh): queen of the Amazons

Reading Selection

Now read this story once, as quickly as possible, for the general idea. Try to guess the meanings of the words you don't understand by the context. You can underline the words you don't know, but don't stop reading.

One day Zeus came down to visit earth and fell in love with a married woman named Alcemena. Nine months later, she had twin sons: One was the son of her husband, and one was the son of Zeus. The son of Zeus was named Hercules (or Heracles) in honor of Zeus's wife, Hera, but it only made Hera more angry. She was an extremely jealous goddess and vowed revenge on the little baby. One night, when the twins were sleeping together in their crib, Hera sent two enormous snakes to kill the infants. As the snakes wrapped themselves around the babies, Alcemena, hearing cries, rushed in to find that the baby Hercules had strangled both snakes to death. She then knew that he was the son of Zeus (but she never told her husband!).

Hercules grew up strong and brave, and when he was eighteen, he saved the people of Thebes from their enemies. The grateful king gave his beautiful daughter, Megara, to Hercules, to be his wife. The two loved each other very much, and Hercules was a caring husband and a devoted father to his three sons. Hera was consumed by jealousy at Hercules's happiness, so she sent a madness upon him. Under this spell of madness, Hercules killed his three sons and then his beloved wife. He awoke, as if from a dream, to see his dear family murdered and blood dripping from his hands. "Am I the cause of these murders of the ones I hold most dear?" he cried. "You were out of your mind," the people said. "That is no excuse. I must kill myself to pay for their deaths," said Hercules. But his friends persuaded him to consult the oracle at Delphi to discover the appropriate punishment.

The oracle told Hercules that to cleanse himself of the sin of murder he must go to his cousin, the king of Mycenae, and fulfill twelve seemingly impossible tasks. These tasks are called the labors of Hercules.

The first labor was to kill the lion of Nemea, a monster who could be killed only by the human hand. For a man who had strangled two snakes when a baby, choking the lion to death was easy. Hercules then cut off the lion's head and skinned the body. Thereafter he wore the skin of that lion as a cloak.

The second task was more difficult. There was a terrible sea monster called the Hydra. It had fifty snake heads, and each head was filled with deadly poison. Hercules cut off one of the heads, only to discover that two heads grew back in its place. Fortunately, he had a friend with him, and, as Hercules cut off a head, the friend put a burning branch to the bleeding neck and no heads grew back. When the animal was finally dead, Hercules put the tips of his arrows in the blood of the monster, knowing that the poison could kill any mortal.

The third labor, while not dangerous, took a whole year. Hercules had to capture, alive, a beautiful deer sacred to the goddess of the hunt and moon, Artemis. The deer became so tired after running away from Hercules for one year, it finally could run no longer.

The fourth task was to kill a wild boar, and, like the deer, it finally gave up from the exhaustion of being pursued by Hercules.

The fifth task was truly horrible. There was a very rich king named Augeas who owned three thousand cows. The stable where the cows lived had not been cleaned in thirty years. You can imagine what it looked like! You can imagine what it smelled like! It was the task of Hercules to clean that stable in one day. But Hercules did not use a shovel. He made two nearby rivers change their courses, and as the rivers rushed through the stable, the water removed all the filth of the cows.

The sixth, seventh, eighth, and tenth tasks were relatively easy for Hercules. He had to save the people from dangerous birds, a savage bull, and man-eating horses, and he had to bring back cattle from a monster with three bodies and three heads.

The ninth labor had a tragic ending. He was to bring back the belt of the queen of the Amazons, Hippolyta. The Amazons were fierce warrior women, but Hippolyta graciously met Hercules and said she would be happy to give him her belt. However, Hera, ever jealous, made the Amazons think that Hercules had come to kidnap their queen. They attacked him, and he, thinking it was a plot against him, instantly killed the gracious and innocent queen Hippolyta.

The eleventh labor was very difficult because Hercules had to get the golden apples of three nymphs, the Hesperides. No one knew where they lived. Hercules went to the guardian of the Hesperides, Atlas, to ask directions. Atlas was a Titan and had been punished by Zeus and forced to carry the heavens on his shoulders. When Hercules asked for directions, Atlas saw his chance for freedom. He told Hercules that if he, Hercules, could hold the heavens, Atlas would go get the apples. That done, Atlas thought he was free forever from the burden of holding up the sky because Hercules now held the heavens. When Atlas returned with the apples, Hercules pretended that he would take on Atlas's burden. He asked Atlas to take the heavens for just one moment, so that he could adjust his cloak to protect his shoulders. Atlas did, and Hercules was able to escape with the apples.

The last labor was the most dangerous and the most difficult. It was to bring back the fierce three-headed watchdog of Hades. To do that, Hercules had to descend into the Land of the Dead and go to the throne of Hades and Persephone. There Hades, the king of the Underworld, told Hercules that if he could capture the watchdog, he could have him. That Hercules did, but when he brought the three-headed guard dog of death to the earth, people were so frightened that he let the dog return to the Land of the Dead.

At last, Hercules felt that he had been cleansed of the horrible murders of his wife and sons. He had many more adventures in his life, always being pursued by the jealous Hera. Finally, he married again, the beautiful princess Deianira. For many years they were happy, but then Hera caused Deianira to fear

Atlas

that Hercules no longer loved her. She gave Deianira a cloak and told her that it had a strong love potion in it. When Hercules came home, Deianira should have him put it on, and he would love only her. But, when Hercules put on the cloak, he felt as if he were on fire. His flesh started to melt, and as he tried to pull the cloak off, his skin and muscles tore off because they were stuck to the cloak. As his blood boiled and hissed, he realized that the cloak had the poison of the Hydra he had killed so many years ago. Deianira, who desired her husband's love, not his death, killed herself in guilt. Hercules begged his friends to allow him to die. He lay down on some wood, and they lit a large fire. The gods in heaven looked down with pity. Even Hera at last felt saddened. "Only his mother's share can perish," said Zeus. "The other part, my part, is immortal, and that part will not die." As the flames consumed Hercules's body, his immortal part was taken up to the heavens and placed among the stars, where you can see him in the night sky to this very day.

Checking Your Comprehension

After reading this story once, what do you think the answers to these questions are? It's OK to guess, and it's OK to not know the answers yet.

1. Why did Hera hate Hercules?
2. What happened to Hercules's first wife and children?
3. How many labors did Hercules have?
4. How did Hercules die?

Be a Vocabulary Detective

Working in pairs, look for hints and guess the vocabulary from the context clues. Then fill in the blanks with the correct answers.

Clue 1

Hera was *consumed* by jealousy whenever Zeus had girlfriends, and she *vowed revenge* on those children of Zeus. She *pursued* Hercules all of his mortal life.

1. To *consumed* means to be _____ (adj).
   a) thinking of nothing else   b) uncaring   c) spending money

2. To *vow* means _____ (v).
   a) to laugh   b) to hate   c) to promise

3. To *revenge* means _____ (v).
   a) to review   b) to get even   c) to reward

4. To *pursue* means _____ (v).
   a) to chase   b) to hate   c) to run away from

Clue 2

When Hercules was just a baby in his *crib*, he *strangled* two snakes that had tried to kill him.

5. A *crib* is _____ (n).
   a) a small chair   b) a large couch   c) a very small bed

6. To *strangle* means _____ (v).
   a) to twist the neck   b) to hit   c) to knife

Clue 3

Hercules's friends *persuaded* him to *consult* the *sacred* oracle at Delphi. The oracle gave him twelve *tasks* to perform to cleanse himself of the sin of murder.

7. To *persuade* means _____ (v).
    a) to convince   b) to argue   c) to disagree

8. To *consult* means _____ (v).
    a) to tell   b) to ask for advice   c) to hire

9. *Sacred* means _____ (adj).
    a) ordinary   b) sinful   c) holy

10. A *task* is _____ (n).
    a) a pin   b) a job   c) a punishment

Clue 4

One of the labors of Hercules was to clean the *filth* from the Augean stables.

11. *Filth* is _____ (n).
    a) food   b) water   c) dirt

Clue 5

When Hercules put on the poisoned *cloak*, he felt that the pain was too much of a *burden* to carry, and he begged for death.

12. A *cloak* is _____ (n).
    a) pants   b) shoes   c) a long jacket with no sleeves

13. A *burden* is _____ (n).
    a) a heavy load   b) a sickness   c) a fire

Questions for Discussion

First, reread the story carefully, looking for the deeper meanings and reviewing the vocabulary. Then in small groups discuss the following questions with your classmates. Be sure to tell what your native culture is.

1. What was your favorite sentence in this story and why?
2. Do you think Hercules deserved to have such a difficult life?
3. Why do you think Hercules was the favorite hero of the Greeks?

Finding the Moral/Lesson

In small groups read the following proverbs and decide which of these proverbs best fits the lesson of this myth. Then share your answer with the class.

a. When it rains, it pours.
b. No pain, no gain.
c. Might makes right.

Now, turn to page 196, find the moral in your list of proverbs, and check it off. Can you think of any other proverbs that will fit the moral?

Double-checking the Vocabulary

Look at the definitions and cross out the words in the list that match. Then, looking at the words that remain, read from left to right, top to bottom, and find the answer to the question, "What did Hercules say to Atlas when Atlas took back the skies?"

a. to get even with someone for something he or she has done
b. extreme dirt
c. an important job that must be accomplished
d. to deeply and seriously promise to do something
e. very holy and pure
f. a difficult and heavy load
g. to convince someone to do or believe something
h. a small bed with rails for a baby
i. to kill something by twisting its neck
j. a long heavy coat without sleeves
k. to be eaten up by something, to be overwhelmed
l. to chase after something and try very hard to get it
m. to ask the advice of someone

vow	revenge	please	crib
strangle	consumed	don't	persuade
consult	task	cloak	sacred
sneeze	pursue	filth	burden

Building Vocabulary from Myths

From this story we get many modern words to describe strength and difficult tasks. Look at the following idioms that are now used in common English. They come from the ideas in the story. See if you can match the items and their definitions. The grammar clues will help. Be sure to turn to page 207 and add these idioms to your mythology and legends word list.

Helpful Note

The Greeks believed that Atlas was the Titan who held up the sky and kept it from falling on their heads. In the late 1500s, a mapmaker named Gerardus Mercator thought it would make better sense if Atlas held up the earth. In a 1595 English edition of his map book, there is a picture of the giant holding the earth, and the title of the map book was *The Atlas, or a Geographic Description of the World.* Some people thought that an earthquake was caused when Atlas shrugged (moved his shoulders).

1. a Herculean effort (idiom)
2. a Hercules (n)
3. an atlas (n)
4. like the Augean stables (idiom)
5. to cleanse the Augean stables (idiom)
6. an Amazon (n)
7. hydra-headed (adj)

a. a disgusting place or situation
b. an evil that multiplies with attempts to suppress it
c. to get rid of filth and corruption
d. an extremely strong man
e. attempting an extremely difficult task
f. a strong, assertive woman
g. a map book

Cultural Notes: Before John Kennedy was elected the thirty-fifth President in 1961, he wrote a book in 1956 called *Profiles in Courage.* In chapter 11 he wrote, "A man does what he must—in spite of personal consequences, in spite of obstacles and dangers and pressures—and that is the basis of all human morality." This is often referred to as moral courage. This theme, that life is not easy, that you have to do difficult and often dangerous things to achieve your goals, and that hard work will be rewarded, is repeated over and over again in American stories, movies, and the lessons parents teach their children. Hercules, also, was faced with serious obstacles and dangers, but once he decided to accept the twelve labors, he never gave up until he succeeded.

Writing

Think, *in English,* about this cultural value of hard work and then, in correct American form and as briefly as possible, discuss the similarities or differences of this value with values in your culture.

Speaking

Share your ideas about this value with the class.

Further Notes: The Night Sky and the Stars

There are currently eighty-eight constellations or groups of stars that you can see in the night skies. Of course, our ancestors could see them too, and in the fourth century B.C., the ancient Greeks named forty-seven of those constellations from characters in their mythology. In A.D. 150 one more name was added, and to this day, forty-eight of the constellations still have Greek names from the myths of the Greeks. If you are interested in astronomy (the science of the stars and planets) or astrology (the belief that the stars have power over our lives) you will recognize these names,

The Constellation of the Crab

for they are the same in most languages, coming from the ancient Greek.

The adventures of Hercules added at least four names to the constellations. Hercules is there kneeling with his club, and the Hydra is the largest of the constellations, looking like a snake covering one-quarter of the sky. In some versions of the story, as Hercules was fighting the Hydra, he stepped on a crab, which bit his foot. Hercules was so angry that he threw the crab to the skies, where you can see it today as the Crab, or Cancer, a sign of the zodiac. Another sign of the zodiac is Leo. That is the lion of Nemea that Hercules killed and skinned. Some believe that the constellation of Orion, the giant whose belt is so bright in the sky, was originally called Hercules. Orion is always pursuing the seven sisters, the Pleiades (but you can only see six of those stars), who were the daughters of Atlas.

Theseus and the Minotaur

Reading Readiness

A.   With a partner, look at this advertisement. Describe what you see. Try to guess the names of the characters in the story and what the story will be about.

TOO MANY UNPAID BILLS? IMPRISONED BY DEBT?

Come out of the maze and into the light with Minotaur Thrift and Loan.

We will consolidate all your debts into one easy monthly payment.

The solution to your puzzle is just a phone call away.

1-777- WAY OUT

B.   Think about these questions and share your ideas with the class.
   1.   Have you ever forgotten anything extremely important? What was it? What happened?
   2.   Have you ever found yourself caught in a shopping mall, on a freeway, in a parking garage, etc., where you couldn't find the exit? If so, how did it feel? What did you do? Share your experiences with the class.

Background Notes

Around 1400 B.C., on Crete, a Greek island, there were many kings named Minos. (You may remember one from the *Daedalus* and *Icarus* story.) They were very powerful. They worshipped bulls and forced the Athenians and citizens of other city-states to make human sacrifices to their god, the bull. It is thought that there really was a king of Athens named Theseus, and so this myth probably began as a legend or hero tale.

Theseus was the most popular hero of Athens, and his story has come to us from Sophocles of Greece and many of the Romans, especially Ovid and Plutarch. Geoffrey Chaucer popularized the story of Theseus in English. An opera, *Ariadne at Naxos,* and several modern novels have been written about the story of Theseus and his battle with the Minotaur. You might enjoy reading two of the more popular novels about Theseus, by Mary Renault: *The King Must Die* (1958) and *The Bull from the Sea* (1962). If you go to Crete today, you can still see King Minos's palace at Knossos. It has beautiful murals of women, bulls, and bull dancing. The famous Labyrinth, however, has disappeared.

Cast of Characters

King Aegeus (*e-jus*): king of Athens
Theseus (*thee-see-us*): son of Aegeus
King Minos (*me-noss*): king of Crete
Queen Pasiphae (*pai-si-fay*): wife of Minos
Ariadne (*air-e-ad-ne*): daughter of Minos and Pasiphae
Minotaur (*min-a-tor*): a beast half man and half bull; son of Pasiphae and a
    bull/half brother of Ariadne

Reading Selection

Now read this story once, as quickly as possible, for the general idea. Try to guess the meanings of the words you don't understand by the context. You can underline the words you don't know, but don't stop reading.

There was once a king of Athens named Aegeus. He had many enemies, so to protect his baby son and heir, Theseus, he took his wife and son to a distant village to live unknown. Before King Aegeus returned to Athens, he placed a special sword and sandals beneath an enormous rock and said to his wife, "When you think our son is strong enough, and ready for manhood, have him try to move the rock and take the sword and sandals. Then he will be ready to join me in Athens and I will recognize him." Theseus grew up strong, brave, and clever. He believed in treating people as they treated others. He admired the stories of Hercules and wanted to become as famous a hero. When Theseus was sixteen his mother told him the truth about his birth and that his father was King Aegeus of Athens. She took him to the rock. Theseus moved it effortlessly and immediately put on the sandals and sword, eager for adventure.

Rather than sailing by ship, he chose to take the more dangerous roads to Athens. On his travels to Athens, he had many great adventures fighting mean robbers on the road. Because of his bravery, Theseus made travel safer for the people and became famous and admired. The first bandit Theseus met had a huge iron club with which he would bash people's heads. Theseus was not very large, but he was very nimble and very clever. As the giant swung his club, Theseus jumped out of the way. The giant lost his balance and fell, and Theseus grabbed the club and bashed in the giant's head. He treated the bandit as the bandit treated the travelers.

The second robber was called Pine-Bender. He would bend down two pine trees and tie the unfortunate traveler's legs to one tree, arms to the other, and then let the trees spring up. You can imagine what would happen to the poor traveler! Theseus used the iron club he had taken from the first robber, hit Pine-Bender over the head, then tied Pine-Bender to the two trees and let the trees go. There was half of Pine-Bender hanging from one tree and the other half on the other! Theseus treated people exactly as they treated others.

As he continued toward Athens, Theseus met a man sitting on a large rock overlooking the ocean. This man was notorious for making travelers wash his feet and then kicking them into the ocean where his pet sea turtle lived. This monstrous turtle loved to eat human flesh. Theseus knew of this criminal, and, as he bent to wash the criminal's feet, Theseus grabbed the wicked man's ankle and threw him off the cliff. Down below Theseus saw the sea turtle eat his last human meal, his master. Just before arriving in Athens, Theseus went to the house of the Stretcher. This evil man would offer his bed to travelers and then tie them down and make them fit the bed. If they were too short, he would stretch them. If they were too tall, he would cut off their legs and head. Theseus wrestled with this monster and threw the Stretcher on his own bed. He fit perfectly, but Theseus cut off his legs and head anyway and then stretched him to treat him as he had treated others.

When Theseus finally arrived in Athens, King Aegeus was told by his jealous mistress, Medea, that this strange young man was really an enemy. As Theseus entered his father's palace, Medea gave him a glass of poisoned wine. Just as he put the wine to his lips, King Aegeus recognized the sword and sandals, knocked the wine to the floor, and hugged his son with delight. The rejoicing was short lived, however.

For many years Athens had been forced to send seven of its bravest young men and seven of its most beautiful young women to the island of Crete. There these fourteen youths were sacrificed to the horrible monster, the Minotaur. Theseus volunteered to go, planning to kill the Minotaur and liberate Athens. Each year the ship that took the young Athenians to their death in Crete carried black sails. King Aegeus made Theseus promise that if he were successful, he would change the sails to white on his triumphant return to Athens.

In Crete the fourteen young men and women met King Minos. The king had been punished by Poseidon when King Minos had disobeyed that god. Poseidon had caused Minos's wife, Pasiphae, to go mad, and she had fallen in love with a bull. The son from that union was half bull, half man. They called this monster Minos's Bull or the Minotaur. To hide his shame, King Minos had his stepson hidden in a labyrinth built by the famous architect Daedalus. Once in the labyrinth, one could never find their way out and would either starve to death or be eaten by the Minotaur. When Minos's daughter, Ariadne, saw Theseus, she fell immediately and madly in love with him. She said she would help him if he would marry her and take her back to Athens as his wife. Of course, he agreed. She secretly gave him a large ball of thread, which she called "a clue" and a sword. She instructed Theseus to attach the thread to the door of the labyrinth and then unwind the thread as he went. When he got to the Minotaur, he would kill it with the sword and then retrace his way to the door by following the clue of thread. And that is exactly what Theseus did.

When Theseus came back from the labyrinth with the blood of the Minotaur on his hands, the other thirteen Athenians were of course overjoyed. They, Theseus, and Ariadne escaped to their ship to return triumphant to Athens. On the way, there was a terrible storm, and they stopped overnight at the island of Naxos. The next day they set sail again. But Theseus did a terrible thing. He forgot his wife and left poor Ariadne asleep on the sand. When they arrived in Athens, Theseus did another terrible thing. He had forgotten to change the black sails of the ship to white. His father, King Aegeus, who stood watching for his son from a cliff, saw the black sails. "I never should have let my son go. Now he is dead." And in sadness and guilt, King Aegeus threw himself down into the blue waters of the sea, which is now called the Aegean in his memory.

Theseus was made king of Athens and was a great and noble ruler. He gave the Athenians democracy and had many more great adventures. It is not known if his memory improved.

Checking Your Comprehension

After reading this story once, what do you think the answers to these questions are? It's OK to guess, and it's OK to not know the answers yet.

1. What does King Aegeus hide under the rock?
2. What does Theseus do to the monster the "Stretcher"?
3. What is the Minotaur?
4. What does Ariadne give to Theseus?

Be a Vocabulary Detective

Working in pairs, look for hints and guess the vocabulary from the context clues. Then fill in the blanks with the correct answers.

Clue 1

Theseus was clever and brave. He *wrestled* with the *bandits* and won *effortlessly* each time because he was so *nimble*. The first bandit tried to *bash* in Theseus' head with an iron *club,* but Theseus bashed in the bandit's head instead.

1. To *wrestle* is _____ (v).
    a) to kill   b) to fight with the hands   c) to run away

2. A *bandit* is _____ (n).
    a) a robber   b) a covering for a cut   c) a musical group

3. *Effortlessly* means _____ (adv).
    a) with difficulty   b) not at all   c) easily

4. *Nimble* means _____ (adj).
    a) quick in movement   b) extremely strong   c) very brave

5. To *bash* is _____ (v).
    a) to hit hard   b) to fight   c) to cut off

6. A *club* is _____ (n).
    a) a group of people   b) a kind of playing card   c) a heavy, thick
                                                                 stick

Clue 2

Because of Theseus, the Athenian *youths* were not *sacrificed* after all. They returned to Athens *triumphant,* and everyone *rejoiced.*

7. *Youths* are _____ (n).
   a) old people
   b) young people
   c) the second person pronoun

8. To *sacrifice/sacrificed* is _____ (v).
   a) to make an offering to a god
   b) to travel
   c) to marry

9. *Triumphant* means _____ (adj).
   a) disappointed
   b) making music
   c) successful

10. To *rejoice/rejoiced* is _____ (v).
    a) to be very sad
    b) to be very happy
    c) to be together again

Clue 3

The bandit who wanted his feet washed by the travelers was *notorious* because he killed the travelers and fed them to his sea turtle, who loved to eat human *flesh*.

11. *Notorious* means _____ (adj).
    a) unknown
    b) famous in a bad way
    c) someone who signs documents

12. *Flesh* is _____ (n).
    a) the soft part of the body
    b) the bones
    c) clothes

Clue 4

The marriage of Theseus and Ariadne was *short lived* because Theseus sailed away without her.

13. *Short lived* means _____ (adj).
    a) lasting a long time
    b) lasting a short time
    c) unhappy

Questions for Discussion

First, reread the story carefully, looking for the deeper meanings and reviewing the vocabulary. Then in small groups discuss the following questions with your classmates. Be sure to tell what your native culture is.

1. What was your favorite sentence in this story and why?
2. Can you explain why Theseus was the most popular and beloved hero of Athens even though he forgot about his wife and abandoned her on the

island and then caused the death of his father by forgetting to change the sails?

3. What significance is there in the story of Theseus and the robbers?

Finding the Moral/Lesson

In small groups read the following proverbs and decide which of these proverbs best fits the lesson of this myth. Then share your answer with the class.

a. Out of sight, out of mind.
b. Do unto others as you would have others do unto you.
c. The bigger they are, the harder they fall.

Now, turn to page 196, find the moral in your list of proverbs, and check it off. Can you think of any other proverbs that will fit the moral?

Double-checking the Vocabulary

Look at the definitions and cross out the words in the list that match. Then, looking at the words that remain, read from left to right, top to bottom, and find the answer to the question, "What did Theseus say to Ariadne?"

a. to hit something extremely hard, especially the head
b. easily
c. someone who robs and steals
d. quick and graceful in movement
e. to fight someone with no weapon but the hands
f. a heavy thick stick
g. young people
h. to give up something important, usually for religion or love
i. successful, victorious
j. to express extreme happiness
k. well known, famous for doing something bad
l. the soft part of the body that covers the bones
m. temporary, lasting a very short time

nimble	don't	wrestle	bandit	forget
effortlessly	bash	club	to	youths
sacrifice	triumphant	set	rejoice	alarm clock
your	notorious	flesh	short lived	

Building Vocabulary from Myths

From this story we get some commonly used words: The most important of those is the word *clue*. When Chaucer wrote the story of "Theseus, Duke of Athens," he used the word *clewe,* which meant, in Old English, a ball of yarn. You can see how the thread or yarn that Theseus followed to lead him back to the entrance of the labyrinth has expanded to become the modern word *clue,* something that will lead you to a better understanding of a problem. Can you figure out the new idiom that is now in style: "I haven't *a clue.* He is *clueless*"? The word *labyrinth* was already discussed in the reading selection of *Daedalus and Icarus* on page 96. It is also clear to see where the name *Aegean Sea* comes from: The water of that sea forms the coastline of Greece and the beaches of Athens. Be sure to turn to page 207 and add these words and these idioms to your mythology and legends word list.

Having Fun

Look at this maze and see if you can help Theseus find and kill the Minotaur.

Can you help Theseus find the Minotaur?

Cultural Notes: One of the most famous phrases from the Declaration of Independence, written by Thomas Jefferson in July 4, 1776, is "we hold these truths to be self-evident, that all men are created equal." This phrase sits in the core of the American mind. If all people are equal then all people must be treated equally: what one does to others should be exactly what one expects others to do in return. "What goes around comes around," is a common American expression. Because of that concept of fairness, parts of the story of Theseus are difficult for Americans to accept. In the beginning of the myth, we meet a wonderful and noble hero whose philosophy is to treat people as they treat others. Then he causes the unhappiness and death of the two most important people in his life. Ariadne saves his life and yet he abandons her alone on an island. He forgets to change the sail and is thus the cause of his father's suicide. Theseus then goes on to be rewarded with a wonderful and full life. The ancient Greeks simply explained this by saying that the gods made Theseus forget. The gods were responsible. To an American, Theseus, alone, must bear the responsibility and the guilt for not treating others as he would have been expected to be treated.

Writing

Think, *in English,* about this cultural value of treating others as you want to be treated and then, in correct American form and as briefly as possible, write about this value and its relationship to the story.

Speaking

Share your ideas about this value with the class.

Oedipus the King

Reading Readiness

A. With a partner, look at this advice column. Describe the situation that is discussed. Try to guess the names of the characters in the story and what the story will be about.

Ask Dr. Burns

Dear Dr. Burns,

I have been married to Charles for four months and am very upset. I'm afraid he is a mama's boy, and I can't stand it. When we first met I was so impressed by how much he loved his mother. I thought it meant he would be a good and loving husband and father. We are in our thirties and it's the first marriage for both of us. He told me he was living with his mother to save money on rent. He called her every day when we were on our honeymoon, and now he calls her twice a day, meets her for lunch twice a week, and takes her to dinner every Friday night, leaving me home alone. Last night he told me how happy he was that his father was dead because now he has his mother all to himself. That gave me goose bumps. Am I over-reacting? Is this normal?

Feeling Left Out in L.A.

Dear Feeling Left Out,

No, this is not normal behavior for a man in his thirties. As Freud describes it, it **is** normal for a little boy to love his mommy and be jealous of his daddy, but the Oedipus complex, a normal stage in the child's development, should disappear by the time the child is about nine. Your husband seems stuck in that stage. You should be number one in his love and affection, not his mother. He needs psychological counseling. If he says he doesn't want or need it, send him back to mama where he belongs and find a more mature man.

B. Think about these questions and share your ideas with the class.
   1. Do you believe that your life is decided by fate or that you have the freedom to choose what will happen in your life?
   2. Name three taboos (something strongly forbidden to do or talk about) in your culture.

Background Notes

This ancient story from Greek mythology is mostly known in America from a Greek tragedy written by Sophocles in the fifth century, B.C. That play, considered the masterpiece of Greek drama (and retold in Latin in the first century A.D. by Ovid), tells the story of Oedipus, king of Thebes, who is fated to kill his father and marry his mother—two of the most universally serious taboos. The tragic consequences of fate and taboos have made this story extremely popular, and it has been retold in many forms—poems, plays, opera—and is the basis of an important theory in modern psychology.

Cast of Characters

Laius (lay-us): king of Thebes
Jocasta (joe-cas-tuh): wife of Laius
Oedipus (ed-i-piss): son of Laius and Jocasta
the oracle of Delphi (dell-f-eye)
Tiresias (ter-ree-see-us): the blind prophet
the Sphinx (suh-fing-ks): a monster with the face and upper body of a
    woman, the wings of an eagle, and the body of a lion

Reading Selection

Now read this story once, as quickly as possible, for the general idea. Try to guess the meanings of the words you don't understand by the context. You can underline the words you don't know, but don't stop reading.

Once, in ancient Thebes, there were a king named Laius and his wife, Jocasta. They had been warned by an oracle that if they had a son, that son would grow up to murder his father and marry his mother. And, alas, the baby they had longed for was a boy. The frightened parents felt that they had no other choice but to have their son killed. King Laius pierced the baby's ankles with a metal spike (just in case he might crawl away) and gave the baby to a shepherd, ordering that the child be tied to a rock on a mountain where it would be eaten by wild animals and die. The shepherd didn't have the heart to do that, so he gave the baby to another shepherd, a servant of the childless king Polybus and queen Merope of Corinth. When they saw the baby with the spike in his ankles, they were saddened by his pain but delighted to have a son. They named him Oedipus, which means swollen feet. They loved him very much, as he loved them, and he never doubted that they were his true parents.

As Oedipus reached manhood, he became famous for his strength, intelligence, bravery, and kindness. Eager to know his fate, he visited the famous oracle at Delphi, where Apollo, the god of truth, had a temple. Oedipus was horrified when the oracle said that he was fated to kill his father and marry his mother and that his children would all suffer terrible lives. Hoping to escape this fate, he fled his adoptive parents and Corinth, traveling in the direction of Thebes. On his way, he came to a place where three roads crossed. There he saw an old man in a wagon being carried by five servants. One of the servants rudely hit Oedipus on the back and told him to get out of the way. Oedipus had been raised a king's son, and no one had ever treated him that way before. At the crossroads, Oedipus struck the servant down. Then the old man and the other servants attacked Oedipus, so he, in self-defense, killed the servants and the old man. Oedipus continued on his way. He met many people coming from the direction of Thebes with horrible news. The king of Thebes, Laius, had been killed, and, to make matters worse, a great monster, the Sphinx, sat on a rock above the gates of Thebes, devouring all who wanted to pass in or out. This monster had the head and upper body of a woman, the wings of an eagle, and the body of a lion. She asked a riddle, and those who could not find the answer were eaten. The frightened people of Thebes were so desperate that they said that anyone who could answer the riddle, and thus save the city, would become king and marry the widow of Laius. As Oedipus approached the Sphinx he saw mountains of human bones. The Sphinx said, "What is it that walks on four legs in the morning, two at noon, and three at night?" "Ah," thought Oedipus, "that is easy," and turning to the Sphinx, he said, "Man. In the morning of his life, he crawls on hands and knees, in the middle of his life he walks strongly on his two feet, and in the evening of his life, he uses a cane to support him." The Sphinx was so furious that the riddle had been solved that she threw herself from the rocks and died. The city of Thebes was liberated, and Oedipus was received by the people as their hero. He was immediately crowned king and lived happily with Jocasta for over twenty years. They had four children, twin boys and two girls. Oedipus was dearly beloved by his people for he was a wise and good ruler, and Thebes prospered.

When their children were grown, however, a terrible plague fell upon the land. The animals died in the fields, the grapes withered on the vines, and the people started to sicken and die. Oedipus sent Jocasta's brother, Creon, to the oracle at Delphi to see what was causing this plague. Creon returned to say that the plague was a punishment for the unsolved murder of Laius. The murderer had not yet been brought to justice. Oedipus, always a man of action, immediately sent for the blind prophet, Tiresias, to find out who the murderer was.

Tiresias could see the past and future, but he refused to tell Oedipus what he saw. When Oedipus angrily accused Tiresias of the murder, Tiresias had no other choice. "You've twisted the truth from me—blind. Though you have eyes, you cannot see. You are the murderer you hunt." Jocasta said not to believe the old blind prophet because oracles lie. She told Oedipus that an oracle had also said that Laius would be murdered by his son and that the son had died when a baby.

Oedipus still wanted to find out the truth, so he investigated further and he learned that Laius was murdered at a crossroads. Then an old servant from Corinth rushed into the court to say that Oedipus was now king of Corinth. His father, Polybus, had just died, and Oedipus was to marry the queen Merope. That would not be a taboo, the servant said, for Merope was not the real mother of Oedipus. He had been adopted. The servant himself had given the baby with swollen ankles to King Polybus.

Jocasta immediately realized that the oracle had told the truth, after all. She ran to her room, pulling out her hair in despair, and hanged herself from the ceiling with her belt.

After he questioned the old servant in detail, the horrid truth finally dawned on Oedipus. The oracles hadn't lied. Humans cannot escape their fate. Oedipus had, indeed, murdered his father and married his mother. He ran to Jocasta, but alas, it was too late. As she hung there in her room, Oedipus grabbed the two jeweled pins that held her dress and thrust the sharp points into his eyes. "What good are eyes to me now? Nothing that I will see can bring me happiness. Apollo destined my painful life, but the hands that blinded my eyes were mine alone. I did it all myself." With blood pouring from his eyes, he gave his throne to his sons and went far away with his daughter, Antigone, to live the rest of his life in punishment for his sins.

Checking Your Comprehension

After reading this story once, what do you think the answers to these questions are? It's OK to guess, and it's OK to not know the answers yet.

1. Why do Laius and Jocasta want to kill their baby?
2. Why does Oedipus run away from his parents in Corinth?
3. What does Oedipus do at the crossroads?
4. What does Oedipus do when he finds Jocasta hanging dead and discovers the truth?

Be a Vocabulary Detective

Working in pairs, look for hints and guess the vocabulary from the context clues. Then fill in the blanks with the correct answers.

Clue 1

The *oracle* warned Laius and Jocasta that their son would do terrible things.

1. An *oracle* is _____ (n).
   a) an enemy
   b) someone who pre-dicts the future
   c) a large ear

Clue 2

They *pierced* the poor baby's ankles with a metal *spike*. Even though the baby was newborn they were afraid he might be able to *crawl* away from the rock. This made the baby's feet quite *swollen*.

2. To *pierce* means _____ (v).
   a) to tie
   b) to put together
   c) to make a hole through

3. A *spike* is _____ (n).
   a) a sharp, pointed object
   b) a small fire
   c) a rope

4. To *crawl* means _____ (v).
   a) to make a loud noise
   b) to move on hands and knees
   c) to kick

5. *Swollen* means _____ (adj).
   a) small
   b) enlarged
   c) cold

Clue 3

Oedipus *fled* from his parents' home in Corinth and learned that, near Thebes, a monster was *devouring* people who could not answer a *riddle*.

6. To *flee/fled* is _____ (v).
   a) to run away
   b) to float in the air
   c) to follow

7. To *devour* is _____ (v).
   a) to end a marriage
   b) to kill
   c) to eat completely

8. A *riddle* is _____ (n).
   a) a trick question
   b) a song
   c) a test

Clue 4

The shepherd did not *have the heart* to kill the baby. Because of that, a *plague* later came to Thebes. That plague caused the animals and people to die and fruit to *wither.* Only the *prophet* Tiresias could see the past and look into the future and tell what was causing the plague.

9. To *(not) have the heart* means _____ (idiom).
   a) to feel sick   b) to be unable   c) to fall in love

10. A *plague* is _____ (n).
    a) entertainment in   b) the beach   c) a sickness of many people
       the theater

11. To *wither* means _____ (v).
    a) to become small   b) to be eaten   c) to become white
       and dry up

12. A *prophet* is _____ (n).
    a) a servant   b) a lot of money   c) one who predicts the future

Questions for Discussion

First, reread the story carefully, looking for the deeper meanings and reviewing the vocabulary. Then in small groups discuss the following questions with your classmates. Be sure to tell what your native culture is.

1. What was your favorite sentence in this story and why?
2. Do you think Oedipus deserved to be punished?
3. Discuss the symbolism of *blindness* in this myth.
4. This is probably one of the few stories from the past in which the parents want a daughter. In many cultures, parents hope for a son and often feel "shame" if the firstborn child is a daughter. The majority of American parents say that they simply want a healthy baby and they don't care if it is a son or a daughter. What is the preference in your culture?

Finding the Moral/Lesson

In small groups read the following proverbs and decide which of these proverbs best fits the lesson of this myth. Then share your answer with the class.

a. Nothing hurts like the truth.
b. Out of the frying pan, into the fire.
c. Forewarned is forearmed.

Now, turn to page 196, find the moral in your list of proverbs, and check it off. Can you think of any other proverbs that will fit the moral?

Double-checking the Vocabulary

Fill in the crossword with the following vocabulary words: oracle, pierced, spike, crawl, (to not) have the heart, swollen, fled, devouring, riddle, plague, withered, prophet

Across

5. a trick question/a game played with words
7. to make something become enlarged, usually through illness
8. (to not be able to) emotionally do something
10. a serious disease that destroys many
12. a person or place where a god answers human questions

Down

1. made a hole with a sharp object
2. eating something completely and fast
3. a person who tells what will happen in the future; a seer
4. made smaller and used up
6. ran away from danger
9. something long and thin with a sharp point
10. to move slowly on the hands and knees

Building Vocabulary from Myths

From this story we get an extremely important theory of psychology. The Austrian doctor Sigmund Freud (1856–1939), the father of modern psychiatry, saw this myth of Oedipus as an important explanation for the normal development of the child. Freud proposed that a little boy's first love is his mother and because of that, the son is so jealous of his father that he wants to symbolically "kill" the father so he can have his mother all to himself. In the Sophocles play, Jocasta "predicts" Freud, for she tells Oedipus that the oracle is just a bad dream and not to be believed. "It has been the lot of many men in dreams to think themselves partners in their mother's bed." Freud called his theory the Oedipus complex. (He also theorized the Electra complex, from another Greek myth, where the little girl loves her father and wants to kill her mother.) Be sure to turn to page 207 and add the names of these two complexes to your mythology and legends word list.

Having Fun with Riddles

In this story Oedipus saves Thebes by answering the riddle of the Sphinx. Here are some popular riddles. See if you can guess the answers and then make up some of your own.

1. What do an island and the letter *t* have in common?
2. How do you make mice very cold?
3. How do you make a cook dishonest?
4. How can you sit on air?

Now, it's your turn!

Cultural Notes: An extremely important ideal in the United States is free will. If our lives are decided by destiny, then we really do not have freedom of choice. Americans typically value the fact that they are the so-called masters of their fate. When Oedipus blinds himself and says, "Well, at least

4. Add a CH and sit down.
3. Add an R and he becomes a thief.
2. Take away the M and they turn to ice.
1. They are both in the middle of water.

I did that myself; that was my choice," it strikes a familiar chord with many Americans. The famous American orator, William Jennings Bryan said in an 1899 speech, "Destiny is not a matter of chance, it is a matter of choice; it is not a thing to be waited for, it is a thing to be achieved."

Writing

Think, *in English*, about this cultural value and then, in correct American form and as briefly as possible, discuss the similarities or differences of these preferences with your culture.

Speaking

Share your ideas about this value with the class.

The Trojan War

Reading Readiness

A. With a partner, look at this advertisement. Describe what you see. Try to guess the names of the characters in the story and what the story will be about.

Declare War on Wrinkles

After just 2 weeks of using Helen of Troy youth face cream, you'll have men beating down your door.

Sold in all fine cosmetic stores and boutiques.

B. Think about these questions and share your ideas with the class.
1. Describe the most important war in your country's history.
2. Describe the characteristics of the most famous hero of that war.

Background Notes

The story of the Trojan War comes to us in English in many different pieces, from several different ancient sources.

The Iliad is the most famous book from ancient Greece. It was written in poetry in twenty-four chapters—called books—probably by a famous poet named Homer. Very little, if anything, is really known about this man except that he probably lived somewhere in Greece, sometime around the eighth or ninth century B.C. The significance of *The Iliad* is not details about the author but its important place and influence in world history, art, and literature. The story, about the war of the city-states of Greece against the kingdom of Troy (Ilium was the name of the main city of Troy, which burned to the ground in 1200 B.C.), begins with the details of a bitter argument between the great warrior Achilles and King Agamemnon. It ends with the death of the warrior Hector and the coming destruction of Troy. The rest of the story, the destruction of Troy, was retold in many Greek plays and in the *Odyssey* of Homer (which you will read on p. 148). The story of the end of the Trojan War came to us in English from Latin translations of the famous *Aenid*, written by a Roman poet named Virgil (70–19 B.C.).

Cast of Characters

On the side of the Greeks
Hera (Greek name for Juno): wife of Zeus
Athena (Greek name for Minerva): goddess of wisdom
Poseidon (Greek name for Neptune): god of the seas
Agamemnon (ag-a-mem-non): king of Mycenae: commander in chief of the
    Greeks
Menelaus (men-uh-lay-us): king of Sparta
Helen: wife of Menelaus
Achilles (uh-kill-ease): Greek warrior
Patroclus (pa-tro-klas): dear friend of Achilles

On the side of the Trojans
Zeus (Greek name for Jupiter): king of the gods
Aphrodite (Greek name for Venus): goddess of love
Ares (Greek name for Mars): god of war
Priam: king of Troy and father of Cassandra and Paris
Hector: a Trojan warrior, brother to Paris

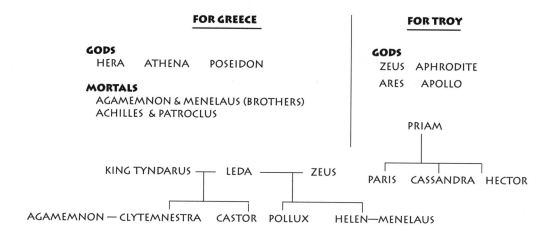

Reading Selection: Part 1—Before the War

Unlike the other stories in this book, the story of the Trojan War is extremely compli-cated and very long. Because of that, this story will be told in three major sections with simple comprehension questions and vocabulary exercises at the end of each. An attempt has been made to keep a lot of the style of the original language.

Now read these stories once, as quickly as possible, for the general idea. Try to guess the meanings of the words you don't understand by the context. You can underline the words you don't know, but don't stop reading.

Homer's story *The Iliad* begins in the ninth year of the Trojan War. The an-cient Greeks were very familiar with the stories of the characters, but for you to easily understand the story, you must first find out what happened *before* the war. You also need to find out details about the lives of some of the most important people involved: Helen, Paris, Achilles, Odysseus, and Cassandra.

Helen: Once, in ancient Sparta, in the land of Greece, there lived a beauti-ful young woman named Leda, who was the wife of King Tyndarus. She was so extremely beautiful that Zeus, the king of the gods, fell deeply and passionately in love with her. He flew down from Mount Olympus in the shape of a swan and made love to her. Soon after, Leda laid two eggs. From one egg came a son named Pollux and a daughter named Helen. These were the children of Zeus. From the other egg came a son named Castor and a daughter named Clytemnestra, who were the children of King Tyndarus. Clytemnestra was as beautiful as her mother, and she was given in marriage to Agamemnon, the king of Mycenae. But Helen was more beautiful by far. She was the most beautiful woman in the world. She was pursued by many princes, and before choosing the man who would be her husband,

King Tyndarus made each suitor swear an oath that if anyone tried to carry Helen away, all the suitors would join together to protect the honor of Helen and her husband (that is, to fight to return Helen to her rightful husband). Of course, each man thought that he would be the lucky one to marry Helen, so they all swore the oath. Then Helen was married to Menelaus, the king of Sparta. (He was the brother of Agamemnon, Helen's sister's husband.) Helen and Menelaus lived happily together for many years.

Checking Your Comprehension

After reading this story once, what do you think the answers to these questions are? It's OK to guess, and it's OK to not know the answers yet.

1. Who was the father of Helen?
2. Who was the husband of Helen?
3. Describe Helen.

Be a Vocabulary Detective

Working in pairs, look for hints and guess the vocabulary from the context clues. Then fill in the blanks with the correct answers.

Clue 1

Because Helen was the most beautiful woman in the world, she had many *suitors*. They all had to *swear* an *oath* that they would protect the honor of her and her husband for the rest of their lives.

1. A *suitor* is _____ (n).
   a) formal clothing   b) a hopeful boyfriend   c) a soldier

2. To *swear/sworn* means _____ (v).
   a) to say bad words   b) to put on a suit   c) to promise

3. An *oath* is _____ (n).
   a) a serious promise   b) a lie   c) a breakfast cereal

Remember that Helen was beautiful, the wife of Menelaus (a king of a Greek city-state), and a daughter of Zeus.

Paris: Paris, the son of King Priam of Troy, was as handsome as Helen was beautiful. Zeus asked Paris to judge who was the most beautiful of three goddesses, Athena, Aphrodite, or Hera. Paris was given a golden ball which he was to give to the goddess he chose. The three goddesses tried to bribe him: Athena offered him victory against the Greeks in war, Hera offered to make him the king of Europe and Asia, and Aphrodite offered him the love of the most beautiful woman in the world. Well, if you were young and handsome, which one would you have chosen? You won't be surprised that Paris gave the golden ball to Aphrodite, making Hera and Athena his instant enemies. Aphrodite took him immediately to Sparta to meet the most beautiful woman in the world, Helen. Menelaus and Helen welcomed Paris as their houseguest, and Paris accepted the friendship and the food and then stole Menelaus's wife. Menelaus immediately called upon all the Greek suitors who had sworn the oath to protect Helen and her husband's honor. They all came with their soldiers to cross the sea and to attack Troy and burn it to ashes. (All the suitors came except two, Achilles and Odysseus.)

Checking Your Comprehension

After reading this story once, what do you think the answers to these questions are? It's OK to guess, and it's OK to not know the answers yet.

1. Who was the father of Paris?
2. What job did Zeus ask Paris to do?
3. Who did Paris choose as the most beautiful goddess?
4. What prize did Paris get after making his choice?

Be a Vocabulary Detective

Working in pairs, look for hints and guess the vocabulary from the context clues. Then fill in the blanks with the correct answers.

Clue 1

The three goddesses, Athena, Aphrodite, and Hera, all tried to *bribe* Paris so that he would choose the one who gave him the best bribe.

1. A *bribe* is _____ (n).
   a) a gift   b) a punishment   c) a ball

Remember that Paris made enemies of Hera and Athena and made a friend in Aphrodite. He kidnapped Menelaus's wife, Helen, and took her back to his home in Troy.

Achilles: When Achilles, the son of the king of the Myrmidons, was born, his mother, a sea nymph, wanted to protect her beloved son. She knew some magic, and so she placed her baby in the water of the River Styx, which flowed in Hades. She knew that Achilles would be protected forever from death wherever the water covered him. She made one mistake. She held her baby by the heel of one foot. On that one small place on Achilles's foot, where her thumb and finger were, the water did not cover the baby's skin. Unknown to his mother or himself, Achilles was left unprotected and vulnerable there on his heel. Achilles grew to manhood and became the most famous warrior of all the city-states of Greece. No weapon could hurt him. When Helen was stolen by Paris, Achilles's mother heard from an oracle that if Achilles went to Troy, he would be killed there, so she sent him away to hide in a king's palace, where Achilles had to wear women's clothes and pretend that he was one of the young girls of the palace.

Checking Your Comprehension

After reading this story once, what do you think the answers to these questions are? It's OK to guess, and it's OK to not know the answers yet.

1. Why did Achilles's mother dip her son in the River Styx?
2. What mistake did she make when she dipped him?
3. What was Achilles most famous for?
4. Why did Achilles's mother hide him, dressed in girl's clothes, after Helen was kidnapped?

Be a Vocabulary Detective

Working in pairs, look for hints and guess the vocabulary from the context clues. Then fill in the blanks with the correct answers.

Clue 1

Achilles's mother dipped her son in the River Styx knowing that the water would protect him from everything. He didn't know that he had one *vulnerable* spot where his mother's finger and thumb had been. Achilles thought he would be the best *warrior* in the world.

1. *Vulnerable* is _____ (adj).
   a) protected   b) unprotected   c) a part of the body

2. A *warrior* is _____ (n).
   a) a soldier   b) a coward   c) a swimmer

 Remember that Achilles was a great and famous warrior and that he had only one weakness, his heel.

Odysseus: The king of Ithaca, Odysseus was wise and good and valiant. He had recently married Penelope, and they had just had a son. He was tired of war and wanted to remain with his family, but he had once been a suitor of Helen's and had sworn the oath to Menelaus. When Paris kidnapped Helen, Odysseus disguised himself as a peddler and went to find Achilles. He pretended to be selling different things, beautiful dresses, perfumes, and some weapons, as well. While all the young maidens were looking at the clothes, one of the maidens picked up the weapons. Odysseus knew that the maiden was Achilles in disguise, and they both went immediately to the Greek camp to join the armies of the other suitors.

Checking Your Comprehension

After reading this story once, what do you think the answers to these questions are? It's OK to guess, and it's OK to not know the answers yet.

1. How many people are in Odysseus's family?
2. Why does he disguise himself?
3. How does he discover who Achilles is?

Be a Vocabulary Detective

Working in pairs, look for hints and guess the vocabulary from the context clues. Then fill in the blanks with the correct answers.

Clue 1

Odysseus was a *valiant* king, but he wanted to stay home with his family. He had to keep his word, however, so he dressed like a *peddler* and tricked Achilles by selling *weapons* along with dresses.

1. *Valiant* is _____ (adj).
    a) frightened   b) very brave   c) expensive

2. A *peddler* is _____ (n).
    a) a wheel   b) a salesperson   c) an old woman

3. A *weapon* is _____ (n).
    a) a tool used to hurt   b) something to eat   c) something wet

 Remember that Odysseus had just married Penelope and that he was wise and good. You will learn more about him in the next story, The Odyssey. *His wife waited for him for twenty years, so you, certainly, can wait to learn more about Odysseus.*

Cassandra: One thousand Greek ships sailed to Troy in an attempt to get Helen back. For nine years the Greeks and the Trojans fought with no one winning. For nine years Paris's beautiful sister, Cassandra, told the Trojans that they were doomed to lose the war, but no one listened to her. When Cassandra was a teenager, Apollo fell in love with her. She resisted his advances but finally told him that she would be his if he gave her a gift. "I want the gift of prophecy," she said. Apollo gave her that gift, and then she told him she had changed her mind—she wouldn't be his lover after all. Apollo was furious at the trick, but the gods cannot take back what they have given, so Apollo kissed Cassandra on the lips and said, "You have been given the gift of prophecy, but since you lied to me, you will foretell the future and be doomed to have no one believe you."

Checking Your Comprehension

After reading this story once, what do you think the answers to these questions are? It's OK to guess, and it's OK to not know the answers yet.

1. Who is Cassandra's brother?
2. Who loves Cassandra?
3. What is Cassandra's fate?

Be a Vocabulary Detective

Working in pairs, look for hints and guess the vocabulary from the context clues. Then fill in the blanks with the correct answers.

Clue 1

Cassandra tricked the god Apollo, and for that crime she was *doomed* forever to have the gift of *prophecy* but to have no one believe the truths she would *foretell*.

1. *Doomed* means _____ (adj).
   a) having unavoidable bad luck
   b) having good luck
   c) having a rounded roof

2. *Prophecy* is _____ (n).
   a) a way to make money
   b) a lie
   c) seeing the future

3. To *foretell* is _____ (v).
   a) to count
   b) to talk
   c) to see the future

 Remember that Cassandra was a Trojan who could predict the future but that no one believed her.

Reading Selection: Part 2—*The Iliad*

Before you begin reading this part, go back to Part 1 and review the *hints* to refresh your memory. Then read this story once, as quickly as possible, for the general idea. Try to guess the meanings of the words you don't understand by the context. You can underline the words you don't know, but don't stop reading.

After Paris carried Helen to Troy, the different city-states of Greece joined armies, and one thousand ships were launched to sail toward the strongly defended great walls of Troy. The war raged for nine years causing the death of many young men. In the tenth year, there was great trouble among the Greek armies. Agamemnon, commander of the Greeks, had stolen a girl-friend of the mighty Achilles, commander of the Myrmidons. In his wrath Achilles refused to help the Greeks. He went to his tent and sulked. At the same time, the gods on Mount Olympus started to take sides. Hera and Athena both took the side of the Greeks. They hated Paris (and therefore

Troy) because Paris had chosen Aphrodite as the most beautiful of the goddesses. On the other hand, Aphrodite wanted to help Paris and Troy, and her boyfriend, Ares, the god of war, agreed with her. Apollo, still in love with Cassandra, favored Troy, and Zeus preferred the Trojans but didn't want Hera to know.

Hoping to end the agonies of nine years of war and killing, it was decided that the soldiers of both sides should rest and only Menelaus, the rightful husband of Helen, would fight Paris, whose kidnapping of Helen had launched a thousand ships and started the war. Putting down their weapons, the soldiers saw Helen watching from a tower. "Who on earth can blame them. Beauty, terrible beauty" the soldiers whispered. Helen turned to her new father-in-law, Priam, and said, "If only death had taken me the day I left my husband, Menelaus, and followed your son to Troy! Now I waste away in tears."

Paris and Menelaus fought with spears and swords. Just as Menelaus was winning, Aphrodite caught Paris up in a cloud and returned him safely to Troy. Agamemnon declared that the Greeks won the war but Hera, who wanted Troy destroyed, caused a soldier to shoot an arrow at Menelaus. The arrow missed but the truce was broken and the Trojan War continued.

Odysseus went to the tent of Achilles to beg him to forgive Agamemnon and fight with the Greeks. "Friendship is much better than deadly vicious quarrels. Let's put an end to them at once." "No," said Achilles "I hate Agamemnon like the very Gates of Death. He is a dog. He cheated me. Nothing will change my mind. I will sail home tomorrow."

Hector, the bravest of the Trojans, went to fight the Greeks. Because the mighty Achilles was still brooding in his tent, Hector ignored the prophecy of his sister, Cassandra, that he would be killed by Achilles. As the Trojans came near enough to the Greek ships to set them on fire, Agamemnon, afraid of defeat, pulled his hair out of his head. Patroclus said to his beloved friend, Achilles, "Enough, let bygones be bygones. Done is done. How can you rage forever? If you won't fight, at least let me go. Give me your own fine armor to wear; perhaps the Trojans will think I am you and give our armies some time to attack."

When the Trojans saw Patroclus, they thought he was the great Achilles and they ran away. Then Apollo helped Troy. In a dark cloud, he tore the helmet and armor off of Patroclus so that Hector could put his spear deep into the bowels of Patroclus and out through his back. "Patroclus, you fool! you thought you would storm my city, but now the vultures will eat your body raw." "Oh Hector," Patroclus gasped, "you won't live long yourself. I see death bring you down at the hands of Achilles." And with those words Patroclus died.

When Achilles heard that Patroclus had been killed by Hector he fell to the ground, pouring dirt over his face and pulling out his hair. "The friend I loved as my own life is destroyed by Hector. I've lost the will to live unless I can knock Hector down by my own spear. I know that as quickly as Hector dies, my death is prophesied to follow. Let me die at once, since I could not save my dearest friend from death. What I really crave is slaughter and blood and the choking groans of men," Achilles cried.

Then a great battle occurred between the mortals, and the gods of Mount Olympus battled each other as well. Achilles stood at the walls of Troy, with Athena by his side, faced by Hector who stood alone, abandoned by Apollo. "Achilles, if I kill you, I will give your body back to your loyal friends. Swear you will do the same," said Hector. "There are no agreements between men and lions, between wolves and lambs. They hate each other to the death. There is no love between us," answered Achilles. They fought and Achilles at last pierced Hector's throat. "I beg you, don't let the dogs eat me. Give my body to my friends to carry home," begged Hector with his last breath. "I wish I could tear your flesh away and eat it raw. The dogs and birds will tear your bone and drink your blood," As Achilles ripped the armor off of the dead Hector the Greek soldiers stabbed Hector's dead body again and again while Achilles made holes in Hector's feet, tied ropes through them, and attached the ropes to a chariot. Achilles then dragged the body of the prince of Troy three times through the dirt around the gates of Troy.

When his rage was satisfied, Achilles dragged the body of Hector to his tent and threw it next to the body of Patroclus.

In great pain and suffering, King Priam of Troy asked for a truce and went to the tent of Achilles to beg for the body of his dead son. "Give us nine days to mourn for my son. On the tenth day we will burn his body and place his ashes in the urn. On the eleventh, we will hold the public feast. On the twelfth day we will fight again, if fight we must." And Achilles agreed to a twelve day truce.

 And so the Trojans buried Hector.

And that is the last line of the Iliad.

Checking Your Comprehension

After reading this story once, what do you think the answers to these questions are? It's OK to guess, and it's OK to not know the answers yet.

1. Why won't Achilles fight?
2. Why does Patroclus pretend to be Achilles?
3. Who killed Patroclus?
4. Who killed Hector?

Be a Vocabulary Detective

Working in pairs, look for hints and guess the vocabulary from the context clues. Then fill in the blanks with the correct answers.

Clue 1

Achilles was in a *rage* at Agamemnon, and he sat in his tent *sulking* like a spoiled child.

1. *Rage* is _____ (n).
   a) strong anger   b) strong fear   c) a large chair

2. *To sulk* means _____ (v).
   a) to show happiness   b) to show a bad temper   c) to creep

Clue 2

Many *sturdy* men had been killed in the *vicious slaughter* of the nine years since the face of Helen had *launched* a thousand ships.

3. *Sturdy* is _____ (adj).
   a) weak   b) strong   c) dead

4. *Vicious* is _____ (adj).
   a) sweet   b) mean   c) delicious

5. *To slaughter* is _____ (v).
   a) to hold   b) to clean   c) to kill

6. *To launch* means _____ (v).
   a) to set sail   b) to sink   c) to eat in the afternoon

Clue 3

When Patroclus died, Achilles felt such *wrath* toward Hector that he promised to run a sword through Hector's *bowels* and let the *vultures* eat his body.

7. *Wrath* is _____ (n).
    a) strong anger   b) strong fear   c) a large mouse

8. *Bowels* are in _____ (n).
    a) the head   b) the chest   c) the lower stomach

9. A *vulture* is _____ (n).
    a) a songbird   b) an insect   c) a meat-eating bird

Clue 4

King Priam was able to stop the *clash* of war with a twelve day *truce* which gave him time to put the ashes of Hector in an *urn*.

10. A *clash* is _____ (n).
    a) a dance   b) a battle   c) a disease

11. A *truce* is _____ (n).
    a) peace   b) war   c) a party

12. An *urn* is _____ (n).
    a) a hole in the   b) a suitcase   c) a container for the ashes of
        ground   the dead

Reading Selection: Part 3—What Happened Next

How are you doing so far? Remember, the war lasted for ten years, and reading this should take less time! You might want to review some of the details before going on. When you are ready, read this story once, as quickly as possible, for the general idea. Try to guess the meanings of the words you don't understand by the context. You can underline the words you don't know, but don't stop reading.

After the death of Hector, the Greeks could still not destroy the walls of Troy. The prophecy, that Achilles would die soon after Hector, came true. As Achilles tried to knock down the gates of Troy, Paris shot a poisoned arrow at him, and that arrow, guided by Apollo, went directly into Achilles's one vulnerable spot, his unprotected heel. The Trojans tried to rip off the armor of the dead Achilles, (just as Achilles had stripped Hector naked), but Odysseus stood over the dead Achilles and the body was taken back to the Greek camp, where they put the ashes of Achilles into the same urn as the ashes of his dear friend, Patroclus.

Soon Paris, who had started the whole war, was killed, yet Troy could still not be taken. Then Odysseus thought up a great plan. He had an enormous wooden horse built that was hollow on the inside. The best warriors climbed inside the horse. The rest of the Greek armies broke camp and pretended to sail away; but they merely hid from sight, leaving only one soldier, Sinon, at the camp. When the Trojans saw all the Greeks sailing away, they came out of the walls of Troy rejoicing. They wondered at the beautiful and enormous horse, and some wanted to bring it inside the walls. They caught Sinon, who, as planned, lied. He said he was an enemy of Odysseus and that the horse was an offering to the goddess Athena. If the Trojans destroyed it, Troy would be destroyed. If they took the wooden horse into the walls, they would be protected by the goddess forever. Sinon explained that the horse had been made as large as possible so the Trojans could not drag it into their city. "Beware of Greeks bearing gifts," one man cautioned, but no one listened, and the horse was taken inside the walls of Troy. Cassandra warned the Trojans that they would be destroyed, but again they refused to listen to her.

The Greeks waited for nightfall, and led by Sinon, they climbed out of the horse to open the city gates where Odysseus and the Greek armies waited quietly. Then the Greeks killed King Priam and his sons, dragged off Cassandra, retrieved Helen, and destroyed the entire city of Troy, even killing innocent women and children by throwing them off the walls of the towers. Helen and Menelaus, reunited again, lived happily ever after.

Troy burned for three years and lay hidden for more than three thousand years until it was discovered in 1870 by a German archaeologist, Heinrich Schliemann. You can visit the ancient site of Troy today and walk among the burned ruins. It is on the northwest coast of the Aegean Sea and the Dardenelles in the country of Turkey. You might even catch some shadows of Achilles, Hector, Cassandra, and Paris, but Helen is probably hiding her beautiful face.

Checking Your Comprehension

After reading this story once, what do you think the answers to these questions are? It's OK to guess, and it's OK to not know the answers yet.

1. How did Achilles die?
2. Why did Odysseus have the wooden horse built?
3. Why did Sinon lie?
4. What happened to Troy?

Questions for Discussion

First, pat yourself on the back for reading one of the most important stories from the ancient Western world. You should be very proud of yourself. Then, take a deep breath and reread the story carefully, looking for the deeper meanings and reviewing the vocabulary. Then in small groups discuss the following questions with your classmates. Be sure to tell what your native culture is.

1. What was your favorite sentence in this story and why?
2. Who was your favorite character in the story and why?
3. Who do you think is to blame for the Trojan War? Explain.

Finding the Moral/Lesson

In small groups read the following proverbs and decide which of these proverbs best fits the lesson of this myth. Then share your answer with the class.

a. Where there's smoke, there's fire.
b. Don't look a gift horse in the mouth.
c. In unity there is strength.

Now, turn to page 196, find the moral in your list of proverbs, and check it off. Can you think of any other proverbs that will fit the moral?

Double-checking the Vocabulary

Fill in the crossword with the following vocabulary words *(some words have been made plural and past tense to fit the puzzle):* bribe, prophecy, suitors, slaughtered, rage, sulk , vicious, sturdy, wrath, bowels, vultures, clash, urn, truce, launch, doom, foretell, swear, oaths, valiant, warriors, vulnerable, peddlers. Four words will be left. With those four words, defined as: predicting the future, extremely brave, a strong soldier, having a weakness, fill in the missing words in the sentence below.

Who dared _ _ _ _ _ _ _ _ that the _ _ _ _ _ _ _ _ _ _ _ _ _ _ _ Achilles would

be _ _ _ _ _ _ _ _ _ _ ?

Across

3. large birds that feed on meat from dead animals
5. attempts to get something by paying money or giving gifts illegally
6. a prediction for the future
8. extremely strong and firm
9. extreme, uncontrollable anger
11. a terrible fate, an unavoidable tragedy
13. to promise to tell the truth
14. to show anger or a bad mood by not talking
15. to cause to begin, especially a boat into the water, a rocket into the sky
17. to come into opposition

Down

1. killed many people or animals, massacred
2. the lower part of the stomach, the large intestines
3. extremely mean and cruel
4. men wishing to marry a woman
6. sellers of goods who go from place to place
7. an agreement between enemies to stop the fighting
10. extreme anger
12. serious promises
16. a container used for the ashes of the dead

Building Vocabulary from Myths

From this story we get many modern idioms. Look at the following idioms that are now used in common English. See if you can match the idioms and their definitions. The grammar clues will help. Be sure to turn to page 207 and add these idioms to your mythology and legends word list.

1. let bygones be bygones (idiom)
2. a Cassandra (n)
3. to work like a Trojan (adj)
4. a Trojan horse (n)
5. to have an Achilles heel (adj)
6. to have a face that launched a thousand ships (idiom/adj)
7. beware of Greeks bearing gifts (idiom)

a. to work hard and never give up
b. to be an extremely beautiful woman
c. to have a weak point
d. something you can't trust; danger from within
e. forgive and forget
f. consider why someone is giving something to you
g. a pessimist

Cultural Notes: In ancient Rome there was a poet named Horace, who wrote in Latin: *Dulce et decorum est pro patria mori*, which means "It is sweet and becoming to die for one's country." During the American Civil War (1861–65), 700,000 soldiers died, and the famous Northern general Sherman simply said, "War is Hell!" In 1918 a British poet, Wilfred Owen, died in World War I, just after writing a poem about seeing all his friends killed in battle. In that war, over 20 million young men were killed. Owens's poem ends with saying, if you had seen what he had seen. . .

> *My friend, you would not tell with such high zest*
> *To children ardent for some desperate glory,*
> *The old Lie: Dulce et decorum est*
> *Pro patria mori.*

On July 8, 1959, the first American soldier was killed in Vietnam, well before the United States had any official relationship with South Vietnam. This war led to great social division and political unrest in America and did not end for America until April, 1975. At that point, more than 58,000 Americans had died. President John Kennedy, who sent advisors to South Vietnam but never authorized any conflict, said in 1961, "mankind must put an end to war or war will put an end to mankind."

Writing

Think, *in English,* about these quotes, choose one and then, in correct American form and as briefly as possible, discuss the similarities or differences of that value with values in your culture.

Speaking

Share your ideas about these quotes and the values that they express with the class.

The Odyssey

Reading Readiness

A. With a partner, look at this advertisement. Describe what you see. Try to guess the names of the characters in the story and what the story will be about.

Fulfill your wanderlust with affordable airline fares and hotel accommodations.

Odyssey Travel, **for all your travel and adventure needs. Fast and reliable service. Guaranteed no waiting. Cruises are our specialty.**

call 1-(777)-ODYSSEY

B. Think about these questions and share your ideas with the class.
   1. In your culture, what are the three most important qualities for a woman to have?
   2. Describe the longest trip you have ever taken.

Background Notes

The story of the travels of Odysseus (he was called Ulysses in Latin), king of
Ithaca, comes to us in English from the Greek and Latin translations from the
famous *Odyssey* of Homer. Like *The Iliad,* the story of the Odyssey has had vast
importance and influence in world history, art, literature, and opera. Many
scholars say that *The Odyssey* is the favorite of all classical stories, for, unlike
The Iliad, which is about the tragedies of war, *The Odyssey* is about the happiness
of finally coming home.

The story is about the voyages and adventures of the warrior Odysseus in his
attempts to return home after ten years of fighting in the Trojan War. It takes
him another ten years to return to his home in Ithaca, to his son, Telemachus,
and his faithful wife, Penelope.

Cast of Characters

Odysseus: king of Ithaca (called Ulysses in Latin)
Penelope (puh-nell-uh-pee): his faithful wife
Telemachus (tell-uh-make-us): his son
Circe (sir-see): a sorceress
the Sirens (sigh-runs): sea nymphs
Cyclops (sigh-klops): flesh-eating giants with one eye
the Lotus Eaters
Calypso (kuh-lips-oh): a sea nymph
Hermes, Zeus, and Athena
Scylla (sill-ah): a monster with a long neck and six heads who stood on a
    high cliff and ate the sailors in the ships
Charybdis (ka-rib-dis): an area in the water that three times a day could suck
    a ship down under the water

Reading Selection

Now read this story once, as quickly as possible, for the general idea. Try to guess
the meanings of the words you don't understand by the context. You can underline the words you don't know, but don't stop reading.

Before Odysseus married, he had been one of the suitors of the beautiful Helen. After Menelaus married Helen, Odysseus returned to his kingdom of Ithaca and fell in love with a beautiful woman named Penelope. They married and had a son, Telemachus. After Paris kidnapped Helen, Odysseus was reluctant to leave his lovely wife and new son, but he had to honor the oath he had sworn as a suitor. For ten long years Penelope waited patiently for her beloved husband to return home.

After the fall of Troy, when Odysseus did not return, people began to gossip that he was dead. Penelope was considered to be a widow and a very attractive and rich one at that! In the seventeenth year of Odysseus's departure, more than seventy men came from all over to ask for Penelope's hand in marriage. Soon the suitors became persistent and rude and moved into the palace, eating the food and drinking wine from the store of Odysseus. There was no one to protect Penelope. She was a woman, alone, with a teen-aged son. For three years she was able to keep the suitors away by saying that she could marry only after she had finished knitting the death shroud for her aging father-in-law. Every day she would knit, and each night she would unravel what she had made so that it would never be finished. Alas, one of her maids told the suitors Penelope's secret, and she was forced to finish the shroud while the suitors watched. Then Penelope had to choose a husband from them. She finally consented to wed the man who could shoot an arrow from the bow of Odysseus through twelve rings.

As the contest began, an old beggar, in rags, appeared at the court, and after all the suitors attempted and failed to bend the bow, the beggar shot the arrow perfectly through the twelve rings. Then he turned the bow and arrow and killed all the suitors. It was Odysseus, disguised, who had at last returned to Ithaca after twenty long years.

Odysseus had had many strange adventures in those years. After the burning of Troy, he left with twelve ships. But the gods were angry at the Greeks and blew the ships off course. After many days, Odysseus and his men landed on the island of the Lotus Eaters. The men who went ashore were given the lotus plant to eat. That magic made them never want to leave, and Odysseus had to tie them up and drag them back to the ships.

Then they landed on the Island of the Cyclops—sheepherding giants with only one eye in the middle of their foreheads. Odysseus and some men went into a large cave filled with milk, cheese, and lambs. One of the Cyclops came in and closed the cave with a large stone. Odysseus greeted the giant and offered him wine, but the giant grabbed two of the men, dashed their heads against the cave wall, ate them, and fell asleep. Odysseus wanted to kill the giant but knew that neither he nor his men could remove the stone from the cave and that they were trapped. The next morning the giant again killed two men, ate them, left the cave with his sheep, and closed the opening with the large stone. While the giant was gone, Odysseus and his men took a huge piece of wood and sharpened the end. When the Cyclops came home with his sheep, again he killed and ate two men. Then he asked Odysseus what his name was, and Odysseus told the Cyclops that his name was Noman. Odysseus offered the Cyclops some wine. He drank it all and fell fast asleep. Odysseus and his men put the sharp wood into the fire, plunged the burning wood into the one eye of the Cyclops, and quickly hid under the bellies of the sheep. The Cyclops roared with pain. The other giants moved the rock, crying, "Who did this to you?" The blinded Cyclops cried, "Noman did this to me." "Well, then it must be from God," they answered. The sheep ran out with Odysseus and his men hiding underneath, and they escaped safely back to their ships.

After several other adventures with giants, Odysseus had only one ship left. Some of his men went ashore on an island where Circe lived. She was a powerful magician and welcomed the men with food and wine. But as soon as they ate, she turned them into pigs, except for one man who was able to escape and warn Odysseus. Aided by the god Hermes, Odysseus threatened Circe with death. She turned the men back to their normal selves, and Odysseus and his men stayed on her island for many months, nearly forgetting their native lands.

At last it was time to go, and Circe warned them to be careful of the Sirens, sea nymphs who could sing so beautifully they would bewitch sailors to jump out of their ships into the sea and death. Odysseus commanded his sailors to put wax in their ears and to tie him tightly to the ship. As they passed the Sirens, Odysseus begged to be untied, but the men, with the wax in their ears, would not listen, and they held their course.

They had to then pass through the zone of Scylla and Charybdis. Scylla was a monster with a long neck and six heads who stood on a high cliff and ate the sailors in the ships. Charybdis was an area in the water that three times a day could suck a ship down under the water. As the sailors watched the sea carefully for Charybdis, Scylla leaned over the cliff, grabbed six of Odysseus's men, and ate them.

They next landed on the island of Hyperion, where the Sun kept his sacred cows. Odysseus made his men swear to not touch the sacred cattle, and for many months they rested in peace. But, alas, one day the men, hungry for meat, killed some of the cattle. As they sat roasting the beef, the meat groaned over the fire, and the skins moved all over the ground. The men ran to the ship, but a bolt of lightning hit the ship. The ship fell apart, and all the men were killed except Odysseus. He swam to an island where Calypso, a sea nymph, lived. She fell in love with Odysseus and offered him immortality, but after seven years, Zeus commanded her to let Odysseus return to his home.

Guided by Athena, Odysseus at last returned home to Ithaca and his faithful wife, Penelope.

Checking Your Comprehension

After reading this story once, what do you think the answers to these questions are? It's OK to guess, and it's OK to not know the answers yet.

1. How many years had Odysseus been away from home?
2. How did Penelope try to keep the suitors away?
3. Who was the beggar who killed the suitors?

Be a Vocabulary Detective

Working in pairs, look for hints and guess the vocabulary from the context clues. Then fill in the blanks with the correct answers.

Clue 1

Despite the ugly *gossip* of the people, Penelope was *reluctant* to allow anyone to become her new husband. Her plan was to knit a death *shroud* for her father-in-law and *unravel* the yarn each night.

1. *Gossip* is _____ (n).
   a) talk   b) insults   c) compliments

2. *Reluctant* is _____ (adj).
   a) having good luck again   b) eager   c) unwilling

3. A *shroud* is _____ (n).
   a) a cloth for a dead body   b) a coffin   c) a painting

4. To *unravel* means _____ (v).
   a) to knit   b) to make   c) to undo

Clue 2

Odysseus knew that the Sirens' invitations to come to them would be *persistent,* so he had his men put *wax* in their ears for protection.

5. *Persistent* is _____ (adj).
    a) loud   b) continuing   c) soft

6. *Wax* is _____ (n).
    a) cotton   b) an earring   c) a soft, oily substance

Clue 3

Some of Odysseus's men killed the *sacred* cows of the Sun and were punished for that crime.

7. *Sacred* is _____ (adj).
    a) holy   b) ordinary   c) expensive

Questions for Discussion

First, reread the story carefully, looking for the deeper meanings and reviewing the vocabulary. Then in small groups discuss the following questions with your classmates. Be sure to tell what your native culture is.

1.   What was your favorite sentence in this story and why?
2.   Do you think Odysseus deserved to have a wife as faithful and as patient as Penelope?
3.   What do you think will happen to Odysseus after he returns home? Will he relax, get bored, look for more adventures, etc.? Explain.

Finding the Lesson

In small groups read the following proverbs and decide which of these proverbs best fits the lesson of this myth. Then share your answer with the class.

a.   Patience is a virtue.
b.   There's no place like home.
c.   Absence makes the heart grow fonder.

Now, turn to page 196, find the moral in your list of proverbs, and check it off. Can you think of any other proverbs that will fit the moral?

Double-checking the Vocabulary

Look at the definitions and cross out the words in the list that match. Then, looking at the words that remain, read from left to right, top to bottom, and find the answer to the question, "What did Penelope say to Odysseus when he came home?"

a. informal conversation about the details of other people or events, not necessarily true
b. important and serious, often religious in nature
c. the cloth which wraps a dead body
d. to undo threads, to clear up a mystery
e. a soft oily substance found in candles and ears
f. continuing in a course of action
g. unwilling and often slow to act

long	reluctant	gossip	time
persistent	no	sacred	shroud
unravel	wax	see	

Building Vocabulary from Myths

From this story we get many modern expressions. Look at the following idioms that are now used in common English. They come from the ideas in the story. See if you can match the items and their definitions. The grammar clues will help. Be sure to turn to page 207 and add these idioms to your mythology and legends word list.

1. an Odyssey
2. a siren
3. caught between Scylla and Charybdis
4. as patient as Penelope

a. to be an extremely patient and faithful person
b. having to choose between two equally terrible choices: also called *between a rock and a hard place* and *out of the frying pan into the fire*
c. a very long and difficult journey
d. a long noise of warning made by a police car or fire truck

Cultural Notes: Part of the history of America is for Americans to leave their childhood homes and families. In 1606, the Pilgrims left their families and homes in England to cross an ocean and start a new life in a part of the New World, which became America. In 1783, after the American Revolution, the pioneers left their parents and relatives in the east and traveled west in search of space, adventure, and a new life. Today, the majority of Americans leave their parents' homes after graduating from high school. Either they start a job or they go to college. Today, few Americans are born, live their lives, and die in the same town. Most travel and set up homes in several different communities throughout their lives. Many change jobs and careers. Most Americans live far away from their childhood friends, cousins, aunts, uncles, brothers, sisters, and parents. Recent statistics show that 18 percent of Americans move every year of their adult lives. After leaving home, the average American will move between seven to eleven times in their lifetime.

Writing

Think, *in English*, about this cultural preference for moving and then, in correct American form and as briefly as possible, discuss the similarities or differences of this preference with the preferred situation in your culture.

Speaking

Share your ideas about the American preference for moving with the class.

Part  3

Building English and Culture
with English Legends

This other Eden, demi-paradise,
This blessed plot, this earth, this realm, this England.
    —William Shakespeare, *Richard II* (1595)

Some say that the age of chivalry is past, that the spirit of romance is dead.
The age of chivalry is never past so long as there is a wrong left unredressed
on earth.
                        —Charles Kingsley, *Life* (1879)

Each evening from December to December
Before you drift to sleep upon your cot
Think back on all the tales that you remember
of Camelot.
Ask every person if he's heard the story
And tell it strong and clear if he has not.
That once there was a fleeting wisp of glory
Called Camelot....
Don't let it be forgot.
That once there was a spot
For one brief shining moment
That was known as Camelot.
            —Alan Jay Lerner, *Camelot* (1960)

A Brief History of English Legends

The ancient Angles and Saxons brought many hero tales with them when they came to England in A.D. 449. These tales were told by wandering minstrels, men who went from village to village singing songs and poetry. One of the favorite tales was about a horrid man-eating monster named Grendel and Beowulf, the hero, who finally killed the monster and the monster's even more horrible mother. This story was finally written down as a poem of 3,182 lines probably about the eighth century. A century before the story of Beowulf was written on paper, a man named Caedmon, "the father of English song," translated some parts of the Latin Bible into Old English in 670. In the ninth century, the Anglo-Saxon king Alfred (849–99) translated Latin books into Old English and called them the *Anglo-Saxon Chronicles*. Perhaps the most important work of the Middle English time is that of Geoffrey Chaucer, who wrote a delightful book of poems called the *Canterbury Tales* in 1387. Those stories are still read and enjoyed today, both in the original Middle English and in translation to modern English.

Why should you, an ESL student, know about this? You need to understand that English has been a language of *written* literature for a very long time. Writing ensures that the stories, and therefore the expressions from the past, will not be lost and that the stories, the language, and the style will remain to influence subsequent generations. English of today still retains pieces from the English of more than one thousand years ago.

The next four stories in *Eureka!* have been chosen because they represent some of the best known and most beloved stories with English roots that are still told and retold in the English-speaking world of today. They all describe the values of *chivalry* and romance. They tell of a time when there were strict codes of manners, when the rich had all the power, when democracy was not known, when a gentleman's job was to protect his king and his lady, and when honor was worth fighting and dying for.

Many of the words in the stories have been modernized to make it easier for you to understand, but an attempt has been made to imitate the styles of the original works.

King Arthur and His Knights of the Round Table

Reading Readiness

A. With a partner, look at this advertisement. Describe what you see. Try to guess the names of the characters in the story and what the story will be about.

Return to Camelot

Step back in time and have fun at
King Arthur's Amusement Arcade.
Joust on the latest video games. Try to pull the sword out of the stone.
Find the Holy Grail. Games and rides for all ages.
An experience fit for a king.
Turn left off Highway 44 at Malory Parkway.

B. Think about these questions and share your ideas with the class.
  1. Do you believe that there is anything worth dying for? Explain.
  2. Have you ever seen a movie or television show about knights in shining armor? Have you ever seen armor in a museum? Describe what it looks like, what it protected the wearer from, and why it is not used anymore.

Background Notes

In England, at some time in the fifth century, there probably was a military leader named Arthur. Some say he was a Celt who fought against the Angles, and some say he was an Anglo-Saxon who defeated the Romans and then ruled the Britons. Stories of this king are found in books from the ninth century. In 1135, during a time of civil wars, Geoffrey of Monmouth wrote a *History of the Kings of Britain,* in Latin. He seemed to tell his tales as a lesson that civil wars will only lead to foreign rule. Since printing was not invented until the 1400s, all books before that had to be carefully copied by hand! We know that Monmouth's book was exceedingly popular for there are still two hundred handwritten copies surviving today! Monmouth's story was translated into French, and it greatly influenced the literature and culture of the French medieval world.

The story of King Arthur that comes to us today was printed by William Caxton, the first British printer, in 1485. It was handwritten in 1469 by Sir Thomas Malory while he was in prison. Malory translated stories from French and added many Celtic legends as well. He named his book *Le Morte Darthur,* the death of Arthur. It comprised more than eight hundred pages and twenty-one books.

The stories of King Arthur had a great influence on the ideas of *chivalry:* a code of bravery, honor, generosity, and kindness to the weak and poor, that the noble soldiers, the *knights,* must follow. We can still see the influence of those stories today in Western art, music, literature, poetry, and movies. Richard Wagner wrote two operas based on the Arthur tales: *Tristan and Isolde* and *Parsifal.* Miguel de Cervantes's *Don Quixote* was inspired by the story of King Arthur. Even the popular science fiction film *Star Wars* was patterned after the story of King Arthur. After you read this story, you might want to see the video of the musical *Camelot* and read the two children's classics *The Sword and the Stone* and *The Once and Future King* by T. H. White and the American classic *A Connecticut Yankee in King Arthur's Court* by Mark Twain.

Cast of Characters

Arthur: king of Britain and head of the Round Table
Queen Guenevere (gwen-uh-vere): wife of Arthur and lover of Launcelot
Launcelot (Lance-uh-lot): one of the greatest knights
Galahad (gal-uh-had): son of Launcelot and the purest of the knights
Tristram (triss-truhm): knight from Cornwall
Isolde (ee-sode): wife of King Mark and lover of Tristram

Merlin (mur-lin): a magician

Sir Ector and Sir Kay: the foster father and brother of Arthur

Mordred (more-dread): Arthur's son

Uther Pendragon (uh-thur-pen-dra-gon): king of Britain and father of
   Arthur

Camelot (kam-uh-lot): the location of the palace of Arthur and Guenevere

the Holy Grail: the wine cup supposedly used by Jesus in the Last Supper—
   legend said that it was brought to England by Joseph of Arimathea

Reading Selection: Part 1

Now read this part of the story once, as quickly as possible, for the general idea.
Try to guess the meanings of the words you don't understand by the context. You
can underline the words you don't know, but don't stop reading.

It happened in the days of Uther Pendragon, when he was king of all England, that he fell madly and hopelessly in love with the lovely and good
Igraine, wife of the king of Cornwall. But Igraine was a faithful wife and
would not look at King Uther. The magician Merlin counseled the king,
and by magic, King Uther made love to the lady Igraine but she thought it
was her husband. That very same night, her true husband was killed in a
battle. Nine months later, when a son was born to Igraine, Merlin named
the child Arthur and took him from Igraine and Uther Pendragon to be
raised by the noble knight Sir Ector.

When King Uther Pendragon died, there was war in the land, for many
knights wanted to be king. Suddenly, one Christmas morning, a great stone
was found in the courtyard of the cathedral in London. There was a sword
stuck in the stone, and in golden letters was written *Whoso can pull this sword
from this stone is rightwise born King of England.* And it happened that many
a knight wanted to be king and attempted to pull the sword from the stone.
Many tried and all failed.

One day Sir Ector and his son Sir Kay, and the young Arthur were riding to the jousts to try their talents with horses and spears. "Oh, I have left
my sword at home" said Sir Kay. "Arthur, could you go back and get it for
me?" "That I will" said Arthur. But when he went to the house it was

locked. "I will ride to the churchyard and take the sword that sticks out of the stone, for my brother, Sir Kay, will not be without a sword on this day" Arthur said to himself. And he pulled the sword from the stone and brought it to his brother. Sir Ector immediately recognized that it was the sword from the stone and, kneeling in front of Arthur, said, "I understand that you must be the king of this land." And he told Arthur of his true birth. Many knights could not believe that such a young lad was to be their king, and for many months they refused to honor Arthur as their true king. They replaced the sword and tried to take it from the stone but only Arthur could pull it out. At last they all recognized him as their true king and knelt down to him and asked for mercy for doubting him. And Arthur was crowned their true king and promised to stand for true justice all the days of his life.

There came a day when King Arthur met Merlin, and they rode into the forest until they came to a lake. In the middle of the lake was an arm clothed in white silk, and in the hand was a fair sword. "The Lady of the Lake will come and tell you what to do," said Merlin. And a beautiful young woman came and said, "Go to yonder barge and row to the arm and take the sword and scabbard." And that Arthur did, and the arm went back under the lake. And Merlin said. "What do you like best, the sword or the scabbard?" Arthur said, "I like the sword." Merlin said, "You are unwise. For the scabbard is worth ten of the sword. For while you have the scabbard you shall lose no blood, so you must always keep the scabbard with you." And that is how King Arthur was given his sword, Excalibur.

And it came time for King Arthur to take a wife, and Merlin said to him, "Is there any fair lady you love better than another?" King Arthur said, "I love Guenevere, for she is the gentlest and fairest lady that I know living." And King Arthur was married to Lady Guenevere and her father gave to his son-in-law the "Table Round" around which 150 knights could sit. But Guenevere's father had only 100 knights to give as a wedding gift. And Merlin went and found 28 more knights, but Arthur would have to wait for the truest knights to fill the other seats.

Arthur and his knights of the Round Table fought noble battles with five foreign kings. They fought for the honor of ladies and to protect Britain. Then Arthur and his knights defeated King Lucius of Rome and conquered Germany and Italy and Arthur was crowned the emperor of Rome.

Sir Launcelot, who loved Queen Guenevere, went on many great adventures for the glory of his queen. And on one he was so badly hurt that he went mad and was found sleeping by a well by four ladies. They brought him to a magic tower where there was the Holy Grail, and they laid him near it, and by a miracle he was healed. When Launcelot returned triumphant to King Arthur's castle, in Camelot, he was acclaimed the first knight of Christendom.

By a trick, Launcelot became the father of Galahad, and many years later another sword appeared in a stone on which was written that only the best and purest knight in the world could remove it. All the knights of the Round Table attempted to do so but without success, until the young Sir Galahad removed it. Now, at last there were 150 knights sitting at the Round Table and it was time to go off on the most important quest of all—to find the magic tower that hid the Holy Grail. After many great adventures, a vision of Jesus Christ came to Sir Galahad, and his soul was made pure from the Holy Grail. Galahad then went by ship to the Middle East, where he was put in prison and, when freed, died in holiness. Sir Launcelot had not been allowed to enter the Grail chamber with Galahad, for his life had not been pure and when he arrived back in Camelot, in the lusty month of May, he forgot the holy lessons of the Grail and began to be in love with Guenevere again.

Guenevere was kidnapped by a traitor, and Sir Launcelot rescued her. He also saved her from being burned at the stake for adultery. Then they lived together at Joyous Guard. Alas, the knights of the Round Table forgot their vows of loyalty and began to fight among themselves; especially King Arthur and Sir Launcelot. While Launcelot and Arthur were fighting, over 100,000 men lay dead on the field. Arthur's evil son Mordred seized the throne. Then there was a battle between Mordred and Arthur, and both were mortally hurt. As he lay dying, King Arthur asked that his sword, Excalibur, be returned to the lake. Then three fairy queens put the dying Arthur on a barge, and they sailed away to Avalon.

Queen Guenevere became a nun and Launcelot became a priest for six years. When Guenevere died, Launcelot never ate or drank again. He sickened more and more and dried and dwindled away, and he died with a sweet smile on his face. They said that he was the truest, kindest, gentlest man to his friends and the bravest and sternest knight to his enemies.

Thomas Malory ended his book with these words (changed for simplicity from the English of 1485):

> *Here is the end of the noble and joyous book that tells of the birth, life and acts of King Arthur, of his noble knights of the Round Table, their marvelous adventures, the achieving of the Holy Grail, and in the end the sad deaths and departing out of this world of them all. Yet some men say in many parts of England that King Arthur is not dead and he shall come again. I, Thomas Malory, will not say that it shall be so, but that here in this world he changed his life. And many men say that there is written on his tomb these words:*
>
> *Here lies King Arthur, the once and future king.*

Checking Your Comprehension

After reading this story once, what do you think the answers to these questions are? It's OK to guess, and it's OK to not know the answers yet.

1. How did Arthur become the king of England?
2. Why did Arthur and Lancelot become enemies?
3. Who saw the Holy Grail?
4. What was Merlin?

Be a Vocabulary Detective

Working in pairs, look for hints and guess the vocabulary from the context clues. Then fill in the blanks with the correct answers.

Clue 1

The stories of King Arthur told of days of long ago when *knights* led lives of *chivalry* and had *jousts* to prove their strength.

1. A *knight* is _____ (n).
   a) the opposite of day   b) a noble soldier   c) a servant

2. *Chivalry* is _____ (n).
   a) a code of manners   b) a fork, knife, and spoon   c) a language

3. A *joust* is _____ (n).
   a) a game   b) a sport with horses and swords   c) a dance

Clue 2

Arthur thought the *lusty* Launcelot was a *traitor,* for he was guilty of *adultery* with Guenevere.

4. *Lusty* means _____ (adj).
    a) handsome   b) full of sexual desire   c) large

5. A *traitor* is _____ (n).
    a) a friend   b) a stranger   c) an enemy

6. *Adultery* is _____ (n).
    a) unfaithfulness   b) faithfulness   c) shyness

Clue 3

Whatever *quest* Arthur went on no one could *slay* him as long as he had the *scabbard* of Excalibur.

7. A *quest* is _____ (n).
    a) a search   b) a question   c) a vacation

8. To *slay/slew* means _____ (v).
    a) to hit   b) to laugh   c) to kill

9. A *scabbard* is _____ (n).
    a) a healing cut   b) clothing   c) a cover for a sword

Clue 4

The dying king Arthur was put on a *barge* and taken to Avalon.

10. *A barge* is _____ (n).
    a) a coffin   b) a bed   c) a boat

Reading Selection: Part 2

Now read this famous love story about Tristram and Isolde, found in Books 8 through 12 in Malory's book of *King Arthur.* As usual, read it as quickly as possible, for the general idea. Try to guess the meanings of the words you don't understand by the context. You can underline the words you don't know, but don't stop reading.

And at this time a certain queen died in childbirth, and they named her son Tristram, for his birth was so sad. Sir Tristram became a great and brave knight and went to defend his uncle Mark's kingdom of Cornwall against the Irish. The knights fought all day, and the blood ran down from them into the ground. Tristram ran his sword into the brain of the uncle of the beautiful Isolde, the princess of Ireland. Then Tristram was badly wounded in battle. Isolde knew magic healing and nursed the handsome knight back to health. Because he had killed her uncle, he said his name was Tramtrist. They fell madly in love and drank a love potion and swore undying love. And when Isolde learned that her lover was Tristram, she didn't care. But, alas, Tristram was ordered to bring Isolde to his uncle Mark as Mark's bride. After many months, desperate for the love they both felt, they met in secret, but Mark caught them and Tristram was banished for ten years. He went to Camelot, where he became a famous and brave knight for King Arthur. King Mark heard of this and went to Camelot to try to slay Tristram, but Sir Launcelot saved Tristram. Later, Tristram went back to Ireland, and he and Isolde escaped to England where they lived happily in the Castle of Joyous Guard. Many years later, and after many great deeds of Sir Tristram, the evil King Mark did slay the noble Sir Tristram as he sat playing the harp for his lady the beautiful Isolde. At that, she fell onto his body in a deadly faint. And all who saw felt a great sadness.

Checking Your Comprehension

After reading this story once, what do you think the answers to these questions are? It's OK to guess, and it's OK to not know the answers yet.

1. Why does Tristram tell Isolde his name is Tramtrist?
2. Who was Isolde forced to marry?
3. Who killed Tristram?
4. Why did Isolde die?

Be a Vocabulary Detective

Working in pairs, look for hints and guess the vocabulary from the context clues. Then fill in the blanks with the correct answers.

Clue 1

Tristram and Isolde drank a love *potion* and *acclaimed* that their love for each other would never die.

1. A *potion* is _____ (n).
   a) a candy   b) a boiled egg   c) a liquid

2. To *acclaim* means _____ (v).
   a) to recognize   b) to deny   c) to swallow

Questions for Discussion

First, reread the story carefully, looking for the deeper meanings and reviewing the vocabulary. Then in small groups discuss the following questions with your classmates. Be sure to tell what your native culture is.

1. What was your favorite sentence in this story and why?
2. In your culture, which figure, mythical or real, is considered the most noble and the most brave? Explain.
3. Why do you think so many events happened by "magic"? Twice there are swords stuck in stones, twice women become pregnant by deceit, etc. Explain.

Finding the Moral/Lesson

In small groups read the following proverbs and decide which of these proverbs best fits the lesson of this story. Then share your answer with the class.

a. All's fair in love and war.
b. There's always a light at the end of the tunnel.
c. If you can't beat them, join them.

Now, turn to page 196, find the moral in your list of proverbs, and check it off. Can you think of any other proverbs that will fit the moral?

Double-checking the Vocabulary

Fill in the crossword with the following vocabulary words: chivalry, adultery, knights, joust, potion, acclaim, slay, scabbards, barges, lusty, quest, traitor, dwindle

Across

5. to become much smaller in size
8. sexual relations between a married person and someone outside that marriage
9. leather or metal covers for swords, usually hanging from a belt
11. a liquid medicine or liquid for magic
13. filled with sexual desire and strength

Down

1. noble soldiers serving a ruler
2. a search for something; usually a very difficult task
3. a code of manners of honor, loyalty, nobility and bravery
4. large, low river boats
6. to announce and recognize usually in public
7. one who betrays
10. an old sport of fighting on horseback with spears
12. to murder

Building Vocabulary from Legends

Besides all the memorable details from this story we get some modern expressions to describe love and chivalry. Look at the following word and idioms that are now used in common English. See if you can match the words and their definitions. The grammar clues will help. Be sure to turn to page 207 and add this word and these idioms to your mythology and legends word list.

1. Camelot (n)
2. a Galahad (n)
3. to search for the Holy Grail (v)

a. a perfect gentleman
b. to go after an unattainable goal
c. a magical place of beauty, nobility, and perfect happiness

Cultural Notes: In 1961, John Fitzgerald Kennedy became the youngest president in American history. At forty-three, he was handsome, well educated, and rich. His wife, Jacqueline, was intelligent, beautiful, and wore very fashionable clothes. His advisors were called the "best and the brightest" in American politics. Kennedy promised hope to a new generation of Americans who were ready and eager to solve the problems of the cold war with communism and racial injustice at home. We were entering what Kennedy called "the new Frontier." In one of the most famous speeches of modern America, Kennedy told the American people to "ask not what your country can do for you, but what *you* can do for your country." He was responsible for creating the Peace Corps, which sent thousands of young American volunteers to help developing nations. He called for civil rights and for defending the defenseless against the tyranny of poverty at home, and against tyranny abroad. It was as if Americans suddenly had a king and a queen to worship, and beautiful plans for a bright new future. And then, just as suddenly, it was all over.

After just one thousand days of presidency, John Kennedy was assassinated in Dallas, Texas, on November 22, 1963. America was stunned. Faith in the future was destroyed. Two weeks later Kennedy's widow, Jackie, told a reporter that the sad lyrics in the 1960 musical Camelot reminded her of her husband's death. Before long, journalists called this new American era, Camelot. And just as England is said to have fallen into a time of civil unrest after the death of King Arthur and disappearance of Camelot, America seemed suddenly thrust into a horrible time after the death of Kennedy and the loss of our Camelot. The bright era of hope gave way to violence, race riots, the Vietnam War, tales about adultery and scandals, and in 1968, the unthinkable: the assassinations of Dr. Martin Luther King, Jr., on April 4, and Senator Robert Kennedy on June 6. Those two leaders had symbolized a possible return to Camelot: a hope for a better world and an end to social unrest. Although it is now over thirty-five years since that day in Dallas, many Americans feel that the country still has not recovered from the loss. For Americans, Camelot symbolizes the end of our nation's innocence.

Writing

Think, *in English,* about this comparison of the story of King Arthur and Camelot to the story of the Kennedys and then, in correct American form and as briefly as possible, discuss if something similar has also occurred in your country's history.

Speaking

Share your ideas about this comparison with the class.

The Legend of Robin Hood

Reading Readiness

A. With a partner, look at this political cartoon. Describe what you see. Try to guess the names of the characters in the story and what the story will be about.

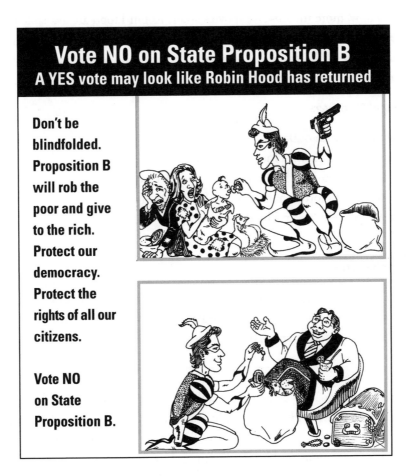

B. Think about these questions and share your ideas with the class.
  1. Do you have any heroes in your culture who were hunted by the police? If so, describe.
  2. Do you have any heroes in your culture who helped the poor fight against the rich? If so, describe.

Background Notes

This old English legend is found in more than thirty ballads and songs. Some think that there really was a Robin Hood, who was born in 1160 in Nottinghamshire, England, a man who was the earl of Huntington, Robert Fitzooth. Others say that there never was anyone like Robin Hood at all. The first mention in writing of the legend of Robin Hood was in 1317. In 1510 a poem of 1,624 lines was written about Robin Hood. Many plays, stories, and songs have told of this hero, and now, more than twelve movies about Robin Hood are available in video stores in America. You might be interested in looking at the 1923 silent movie *Robin Hood*, the 1976 *Robin and Marian*, starring Sean Connery and Audrey Hepburn, and the 1991 Kevin Costner film, *Robin Hood, Prince of Thieves*.

Cast of Characters

Robin Hood: an outlaw
Maid Marian: Robin Hood's girlfriend
Little John and Friar Tuck: Robin Hood's friends
the sheriff of Nottingham: Robin Hood's enemy
the merry men: Robin Hood's followers

Reading Selection

Now read this story once, as quickly as possible, for the general idea. Try to guess the meanings of the words you don't understand by the context. You can underline the words you don't know, but don't stop reading.

Once, long ago, in Nottingham, England, there lived a young and carefree man named Robin Hood. When he wasn't visiting his girlfriend, the maid Marian, he liked nothing better than to be with his friends and to go hunting. He was famous for his talent with his bow and arrow and his excellent aim. One day, when he and his friends were hunting in the forest of Sherwood, Robin shot a deer. Unfortunately for the deer, and Robin as well, the animal belonged to the king. Because of that, one of the king's guards tried to kill Robin. In self-defense, Robin killed the guard. The sheriff of Nottingham vowed to bring Robin to justice for the murder, so Robin had to flee deep into the forest, where he was forced to live as an outlaw. He knew he would never see Marian again, but he had no choice. His friends went with him, and soon many men whose lives were in danger or who just wanted their freedom to live as they pleased joined Robin Hood's band of merry men in Sherwood Forest.

Robin was always eager to test his fighting prowess, and the men who could defeat Robin became his best friends. One day Robin was about to cross a river that had a very narrow bridge. On the bridge was a man seven feet tall who would not allow Robin to pass. The two fought with long stout sticks, and the tall man threw Robin into the river. Robin Hood was not ashamed or angry. He immediately congratulated the tall man and invited him to become a member of his band of men. They called the man Little John, and he became Robin Hood's right-hand man. Robin Hood's other good friend was a fat and happy monk whose name was Friar Tuck.

Whenever Robin Hood and his men heard of trouble in the area, they would go to defend the innocent and fight for justice. They often stole from the rich to give to the poor, and they defended the honor of women and protected the lives of children.

The sheriff of Nottingham however, was always looking for Robin, so Robin often wore a disguise. One day, in disguise, he met a young man in the forest. They fought with swords, and Robin became impressed by the valor of his foe. Robin congratulated the young man on his talents, and the young man, recognizing the voice of Robin Hood, threw down the sword and rushed to Robin's arms. It was Maid Marian, who had gone into Sherwood Forest disguised as a man to look for her love.

Robin, Marian, Little John, Friar Tuck, and the merry men all lived in the forest for many years, hiding from the sheriff and fighting for justice for the poor and needy. They had many adventures and were never defeated by mortal men. But, alas, Time, that enemy of all, led to the defeat of Robin Hood. When Robin got old he became very sick. He went to the Church of Kirklees, where a nun, who was a famous nurse, lived. He asked her to cure his illness. In those days, doctors would "bleed" their patients, which means they would make a small cut in the skin and remove some blood, thinking that would cure the disease by releasing the poisons from the body. The nun was, however, a friend of the sheriff of Nottingham and a secret enemy of Robin Hood, so she "bled" him, but she didn't stop the bleeding, and the valiant Robin Hood bled to death.

Today, you can visit the ruins of Kirklees Priory in Yorkshire, England, and you will see a grave. On the tombstone are written these words:

> *Here underneath this little stone*
> *Lies Robert, Earl of Huntingdon.*
> *There never was an archer so good*
> *And people called him Robin Hood.*
> *Such outlaws as he and his men*
> *England will never see again.*
> *died: 1247*

Checking Your Comprehension

After reading this story once, what do you think the answers to these questions are? It's OK to guess, and it's OK to not know the answers yet.

1. Why did Robin Hood become an outlaw?
2. How did Robin meet Maid Marian after he fled to the forest?
3. How did Robin die?

Be a Vocabulary Detective

Working in pairs, look for hints and guess the vocabulary from the context clues. Then fill in the blanks with the correct answers.

Clue 1

Robin Hood was a *carefree* young man until he shot the king's deer with his *bow* and arrow. Then he had to *flee* into the forest, where he was forced to become an *outlaw*.

1. *Carefree* is _____ (adj).
   a) serious   b) easygoing   c) unreliable

2. A *bow* is shaped like _____ (n).
   a) a circle   b) a straight line   c) a new moon

3. To *flee* means _____ (v).
   a) to float in the air b) to sit down   c) to run away

4. An *outlaw* is _____ (n).
   a) a criminal   b) related by marriage   c) an innocent person

Clue 2

Robin Hood *vowed* to help the poor with his *valiant* friends. When they hunted, they had perfect *aim,* and they showed great *prowess* in all that they did.

5. To *vow* is _____ (v).
    a) to lie   b) to promise   c) to hunt

6. *Valiant* is _____ (adj).
    a) cowardly   b) handsome   c) brave

7. To *aim* means _____ (v).
    a) to miss   b) to try to hit   c) to desire

8. *Prowess* is _____ (n).
    a) bravery   b) cowardice   c) walking softly

Clue 3

Robin Hood's *right-hand* man was Little John. He was tall and *stout* and fought his *foes* without needing a *disguise.*

9. *A right-hand* man is _____ (idiom/n).
    a) the most valuable   b) not left handed   c) unreliable

10. *Stout* is _____ (adj).
    a) weak   b) thin   c) fat

11. A *foe* is _____ (n).
    a) a friend   b) an enemy   c) a stranger

12. *Disguise* is _____ (n).
    a) a shirt   b) a hat   c) a mask

Questions for Discussion

First, reread the story carefully, looking for the deeper meanings and reviewing the vocabulary. Then in small groups discuss the following questions with your classmates. Be sure to tell what your native culture is.

1. What was your favorite sentence in this story and why?
2. Do you think Robin Hood deserves to be considered a hero?
3. Do you think the sheriff of Nottingham was right or wrong to be the enemy of Robin Hood?

Finding the Moral/Lesson

In small groups read the following proverbs and decide which of these proverbs best fits the lesson of this story. Then share your answer with the class.

a. Two wrongs don't make a right.
b. It is more blessed to give than to receive.
c. Don't judge a man until you've walked in his shoes.

Now, turn to page 196, find the moral in your list of proverbs, and check it off. Can you think of any other proverbs that will fit the moral?

Double-checking the Vocabulary

Fill in the crossword with the following vocabulary words: carefree, bow, aim, vow, flee, outlaw, prowess, stout, valiant, right hand man, disguise, foe, Maid Marian.

Across

1. the name of Robin Hood's girlfriend
8. fat, thick, or strong
9. criminal, one wanted by the authorities
10. easygoing, lighthearted, having no problems in life
11. an enemy
12. acting with great bravery, possessing valor

Down

2. to try to hit a certain mark
3. an attempt to hide one's identity
4. the most valuable person to another, reliable and responsible
5. skill
6. a piece of wood, held in a curve by a tight string, for shooting arrows
7. to run away because of danger
12. an extremely serious promise

Cultural Notes: In the United States there is a tendency to admire the triumph of good over evil, the weak over the strong, and the poor over the rich. Our country's heroes have often come from the bottom and worked their way up to the top. They fought for what they believed was right; they fought to protect the rights of the average person. Besides Robin Hood, modern examples of this type of hero would be the cartoon heroes Superman, Batman, Wonder Woman, Spiderman, the Green Hornet, the Lone Ranger, etc. More recently, in the movies and on television, there are heroes like Colombo, Luke Skywalker, Indiana Jones, Forrest Gump, and, of course, the heroes of the cowboy movies of the past fifty years.

Writing

Think, *in English,* about these heroes and then, in correct American form and as briefly as possible, discuss the similarities or differences of these heroes with heroes in your culture.

Speaking

Share your ideas about these values with the class.

Lady Godiva

Reading Readiness

A.   With a partner, look at this advertisement. Describe what you see. Try to guess the names of the characters in the story and what the story will be about.

> # Make your hair your crowning glory
> # Godiva Hair Care Products
>
> ### Everyone will be peeping at the new, gorgeous you.
>
> *Sold in all fine salons and beauty supply stores.*

B.   Think about these questions and share your ideas with the class.
1.   Can you think of any circumstance in which you would be willing to embarrass yourself if it would help someone in need? If so, explain.
2.   Describe the qualities of a famous heroine in your culture.

Background Notes

The legend of Lady Godiva was first written down in England in the 1200s and later rewritten by a man named Rapin in his *History of England* in 1723. The story has been the subject of many poems, paintings, and statues, as well as costumes at Halloween parties! Since 1768, there has been an annual Lady Godiva festival in the city of Coventry in England.

Cast of Characters

Leofric (lee-oh-frick): lord of Coventry, England
Lady Godiva (guh-die-va): wife of Leofric
Peeping Tom: a tailor

Reading Selection

Now read this story once, as quickly as possible, for the general idea. Try to guess the meanings of the words you don't understand by the context. You can underline the words you don't know, but don't stop reading.

Once, in the year 1040 in England, there lived a very shy and modest woman named Lady Godiva. Her husband's name was Leofric, and he was the ruler of the city of Coventry. Lord Leofric was extremely rich and owned all of the land of the town and the farms. He was greedy and decided he could make much more money if he forced his tenants to pay even more taxes. The people did not know what to do since they were already struggling to put food on the table; to pay more taxes meant certain starvation. They decided to send a representative to Lady Godiva to ask for help. The good lady was heartbroken to hear of their plight and immediately went to her husband to beseech him to have pity and compassion for his tenants. "Oh, so your heart is breaking for those people, my dear," he sneered. "I know how shy you are. I dare you to prove how sincere your feelings are. If you ride through the town square, naked, at high noon, then and only then will I lower the taxes."

Lady Godiva thought she would die from embarrassment, but she decided that if her actions could keep one stomach full and one child from dying, it would be well worth it. All the people heard that their benefactress would save them from certain poverty by riding down the main streets of town with nothing to cover her body but her long, golden hair. In respect and love for her kind sacrifice, they all promised to stay inside with their shutters tightly closed. And they all did, except for one man, a tailor named Tom, who let his curiosity get the better of him and he peeked out his shutters to see Lady Godiva naked. By some miracle, he was immediately struck blind. Lord Leofric, seeing how deeply his wife cared for her people, did, indeed keep his word, and the people of Coventry loved and blessed their dear, gracious Lady Godiva until the day she died.

Checking Your Comprehension

After reading this story once, what do you think the answers to these questions are? It's OK to guess, and it's OK to not know the answers yet.

1. Why did Leofric raise the taxes?
2. Why did Lady Godiva ride through the town naked?
3. What happened to Tom when he looked out the shutters?

Be a Vocabulary Detective

Working in pairs, look for hints and guess the vocabulary from the context clues. Then fill in the blanks with the correct answers.

Clue 1

Lord Leofric was so *greedy* that he wanted to raise the taxes, causing the possibility of *starvation* among the poor.

1. *Greedy* means _____ (adj).
    a) dangerous   b) angry   c) always wanting more

2. *Starvation* is _____ (n).
    a) severe hunger   b) severe thirst   c) severe cold

Clue 2

The poor people were in a terrible *plight* and *beseeched* Lady Godiva to help them. She *sacrificed* her modesty to become their *benefactress*.

3. *Plight* is _____ (n).
    a) a serious condition   b) great fear   c) great hunger

4. To *beseech* means _____ (v).
   a) to argue   b) to beg   c) to cry

5. To *sacrifice* means _____ (v).
   a) to put on   b) to take off   c) to give something up

6. A *benefactress* is _____ (n).
   a) an actress   b) a woman who does good   c) a woman who is modest

Clue 3

Leofric thought his wife would never take off her clothes in public, and he *sneered* when he *dared* her to ride through the town, naked at *high noon.*

7. To *sneer* means _____ (v).
   a) to make fun of   b) to frown   c) to cry

8. To *dare* means _____ (v).
   a) to decide   b) to challenge   c) to disagree

9. *High noon* is _____ (n).
   a) exactly at 12:00 P.M.   b) midnight   c) during the full moon

Clue 4

Unlike all the other townspeople, who closed their *shutters* tight, Tom *peeked* out the window to see Lady Godiva.

10. A *shutter* is _____ (n).
    a) glass   b) a screen   c) a window covering to keep out the light

11. To *peek* means _____ (v).
    a) to laugh   b) to look   c) to cry

Questions for Discussion

First, reread the story carefully, looking for the deeper meanings and reviewing the vocabulary. Then in small groups discuss the following questions with your classmates. Be sure to tell what your native culture is.

1. What was your favorite sentence in this story and why?
2. Do you think that Tom deserved his punishment?
3. Do you think Leofric was a good husband or a bad husband? Explain.

Finding the Moral/Lesson

In small groups read the following proverbs and decide which of these proverbs best fits the lesson of this story. Then share your answer with the class.

a. Seeing is believing.
b. One good turn deserves another.
c. A friend in need is a friend indeed.

Now, turn to page 196, find the moral in your list of proverbs, and check it off. Can you think of any other proverbs that will fit the moral?

Double-checking the Vocabulary

Look at the definitions and cross out the words in the list that match. Then, looking at the words that remain, read from left to right, top to bottom, and find the answer to the question, "What was Lady Godiva wearing?"

a. a woman who does good deeds
b. a sad, sorrowful, and serious condition
c. wanting much more than one needs
d. to make fun of someone because you disapprove, a mean smile
e. exactly on the stroke of 12:00 P.M.
f. extreme hunger
g. to give up something important and valuable for a religious or moral cause
h. to beg for something, ask for something with deep emotion
i. metal or wooden window coverings to keep out light, noise, or weather
j. to look at something quickly and secretly, especially when you shouldn't

greedy	starvation	she	plight
was	beseech	wearing	sneer
high noon	her	benefactress	sacrifice
peek	birthday	shutters	suit

Building Vocabulary from Legends

From this story we get three modern expressions. Look at the following idioms that are now used in common English. They come from the ideas in the story. See if you can match the items and their definitions. Be sure to turn to page 207 and add these idioms to your mythology and legends word list.

1. She could be a Lady Godiva.
2. A peeking (sometimes *peeping*) Tom.
3. To be sent to Coventry.

a. a person who likes to secretly look at people, usually of the opposite sex, and especially at people who are getting dressed or undressed
b. nobody will talk to you (because they disapprove of what you have done)
c. an extremely beautiful woman

Cultural Notes: The right to privacy and the right to fair taxation have been important issues in the culture and the laws of the United States since colonial times. In 1776 the thirteen colonies declared their independence (and therefore started a revolution) from England for many reasons. Two of those reasons were: (1) that King George III of England had taken away the privacy of the colonists by allowing British officers to search personal property and live and eat in people's homes without their permission, and (2) that the king had taxed the colonists without allowing the colonists to have any say in being taxed or to receive any benefits from those taxes. Later, in 1791, after the colonies became the United States, laws called the Bill of Rights were added to make the Constitution (the supreme law of the land) more clear. Amendment 4 is often called the right to privacy. It guarantees a right to complete privacy for all people, including children. Not even the police can enter your home or gather personal information without permission from the court. This idea of privacy extends even further into Americans' sense of personal space. You might have noticed that most Americans do not like to be closer to others than eighteen inches, and they might get very upset if someone (even their mother, wife or husband) reads their mail or listens in to their telephone conversation. This idea of privacy can even extend to Americans' desire to fairly control their own money and property. The colonists questioned how much money a government deserves and what benefits the citizens will get from that money. In 1787 the Constitution stated that the government had the power to collect taxes but those taxes must be equal throughout the United States. This idea about fair taxation was further clarified in 1913 by Amendment 16, which allows the government to collect taxes based on people's incomes.

Writing

Think, *in English,* about this preference for personal privacy and then, in correct American form and as briefly as possible, discuss the similarities or differences of this preference with attitudes about privacy in your culture.

Speaking

Share your ideas about this preference for privacy with the class.

Romeo and Juliet

Reading Readiness

A. With a partner, look at this advertisement. Describe what you see. Try to guess the names of the characters in the story and what the story will be about.

B. Look at these questions and share your ideas with the class.
1. Do you believe in love at first sight? If yes, do you think it usually lasts?
2. What is your opinion about lovers who go against their parents' wishes and marry someone the parents consider an enemy?

Background Notes

William Shakespeare (1564–1616) is the most important and the best-known writer in English literature. He wrote over 37 plays and more than 160 poems that are still performed and read to this day. Perhaps his work has lasted over four hundred years because of his deep understanding of human nature, which enabled him to write of the universal human emotions of love, pain, jealousy, anger, and hatred. He is also known as having used the English language in new and unique ways, of creating new words, and having a sense of the music of the language. He is the most famous writer in English and known throughout the world. For the ESL student, Shakespeare is particularly important because he created over 1,700 new words and contributed hundreds of new sayings to English: words and expressions which have been used for four hundred years and are still used today in common, everyday speech. Shakespeare said he was "a man of fire-new words" who loved to experiment with putting words together. He used over 30,000 words in his works (the average educated person of today uses no more 15,000 words). An example of a few of Shakespeare's created words commonly used today are: radiance, dwindle, monumental, majestic, excellent, hint, hurry, lonely, homicide, assassination, and fragrant. Familiar expressions from Shakespeare are: snow-white, flesh and blood, vanish into thin air, tower of strength, too much of a good thing, and to have seen better days.

Shakespeare wrote the tragic romance of *Romeo and Juliet* in 1596, adapted from a poem written in English in 1562, which had been adapted from earlier Italian and French poems.

The story of Romeo and Juliet has been found often in poems, ballet, opera, art, and movies. After you read the original story, you might want to watch some of the film adaptations of the play: the classic 1936 black and white film, the 1968 Franco Zeffirelli version in which the actors were young teenagers themselves, and the 1997 version of *Romeo and Juliet* set in modern times. You might also like to watch the 1961 musical *Westside Story*, a modern Romeo and Juliet, about rival Puerto Rican and white youth gangs in New York.

Reading Shakespeare in the original Elizabethan English is extremely difficult for even the most advanced ESL student. You'll be able to find many edited versions in modern English, and it will enrich your knowledge of English and culture to read some of his famous plays, especially *Hamlet, Twelfth Night, King Lear, Julius Caesar,* and, of course, *Romeo and Juliet.* In the version you will now read, most of the lines in the quotation marks are from the original 1596 play. A few of the words have been modernized to make the story easier for you to understand.

Cast of Characters

the Montagues (mon-ta-gyous) and the Capulets (cap-you-lets): two rich
   families in Verona, (ver-own-uh), Italy
Romeo (ro-me-o) Montague: a young man
Juliet Capulet: a young woman (actually, she is only thirteen!)
Friar Laurence: a monk
the nurse: Juliet's trusted maid
Mercutio (mer-cue-she-o) and Benvolio (ben-vo-lee-o): friends of Romeo
Tybalt: (ti-ball-t) Juliet's cousin
Count Paris: a young nobleman

Reading Selection

Now read this story once, as quickly as possible, for the general idea. Try to guess
the meanings of the words you don't understand by the context. You can underline the words you don't know, but don't stop reading.

Once in the town of Verona, there lived two rich families, the Montagues
and the Capulets. For reasons long forgotten, these two families hated each
other and were sworn enemies.

One night, Lord Capulet gave a grand ball. Romeo Montague heard
that Rosaline, who had refused to be his girlfriend, would be at the dance.
Although it was forbidden and dangerous for a Montague to go to the
house of a Capulet, Romeo went with his friends Benvolio and Mercutio,
all in disguise. It was at this party that Romeo first saw Juliet Capulet. To
his eyes, she was the most beautiful woman in the world. He immediately
forgot his love for Rosaline. "Did my heart love till now?" he asked himself. "I never saw true beauty till this night." As Romeo and Juliet's eyes
met, they rushed to each other and fell head over heels in love. They kissed,
and when Romeo left, Juliet asked her nurse who the man in the disguise
was. "His name is Romeo and a Montague. The only son of your great enemy." "My only love sprung from my only hate! Too early seen unknown,
and known too late!" Juliet said in sadness. She ran upstairs to her bedroom
and went out to look at the night sky from her balcony. Romeo had hidden
in her garden and saw Juliet come out the balcony window. "What light
through yonder window breaks?" he whispered to himself. "It is the east
and Juliet is the sun." Romeo thought that the poor moon was pale and

jealous of the beauty of Juliet and that "the brightness of her cheek would shame the stars. Oh, see how she leans her cheek upon her hand. Oh! that I were a glove upon that hand, that I might touch that cheek!"

Juliet, thinking she was alone, talked to herself, "Oh Romeo, Romeo, wherefore art thou (why are you) Romeo? Refuse your name. . . . It is but your name that is my enemy. You are yourself, though not a Montague. What's a Montague? What's in a name? That which we call a rose by any other word would smell as sweet." Romeo and Juliet then exchanged vows of love and promised to marry the next day, their love for each other was as deep as the sea. Saying good-bye was painful to them: "Good night, good night! Parting is such sweet sorrow, that I shall say goodnight until it be tomorrow."

At daybreak, Romeo left Juliet's garden and ran to his religious advisor, Friar Laurence, to ask for help in marrying Juliet. The friar thought that a marriage between a Capulet and a Montague could turn the hatred of the two households into pure love, and so he consented to join the hands of Romeo and Juliet in marriage. Juliet's trusted nurse was told of the plan, and as Juliet rushed to the monastery to be married, the nurse went to find a ladder so that the new husband, Romeo, could climb up to Juliet's bedroom for their wedding night.

But, alas, the lovers were truly star-crossed and fated to unhappiness. That afternoon, just after the marriage, Romeo, Mercutio, and Benvolio were walking on the city streets. Unfortunately they were met by Juliet's cousin, Tybalt, and a group of Capulets. Tybalt knew that Romeo had been at the Capulet ball the night before, and he was very angry. Romeo did not want to fight with his new cousin, but Tybalt drew his sword and killed Mercutio. Romeo killed Tybalt. The prince of Verona arrived on the scene and immediately banished Romeo from Verona to Mantua. "Oh, I am Fortune's fool!" cried Romeo, running to Friar Laurence's. "There is no world outside of Verona. This banishment is death. This is Hell," he said. "Heaven is here in Verona, where Juliet lives, and every cat and dog and little mouse, every unworthy thing lives here in Heaven and may look on her: but Romeo may not." The friar counseled Romeo that all would end well and that it was time to go to his bride. The newlyweds spent a beautiful night together and were deeply saddened by the coming morning. Juliet tried to deny that it was the sun rise. "It must be a meteor that lights the sky." She begged Romeo to stay. "I must be gone and live or stay and die," he said. As Romeo crawled out of the balcony window, Juliet's mother came to tell her that the

Capulets had decided that in two days Juliet would be married to Count Paris.

In despair, Juliet ran to Friar Laurence's, and he told her of his plan to save her marriage. She must agree to marry Paris so that no one would become suspicious. Then she was to drink the medicine he gave her. Friar Laurence told her to not be too afraid. The medicine would make her fall into a deep sleep for forty-two hours. Her parents would think she was dead and take her to the family tomb. At the same time, Friar Laurence would send a messenger to Romeo, who would come and take her away with him to Mantua. "Give me, give me, tell me not of fear. Love will give me strength," she said as she took the bottle.

The next morning when the nurse went to wake Juliet, she appeared to be dead. "Death lies on her like an untimely frost upon the sweetest flower of all the field. Oh day! Oh hateful day! Never was seen so black a day as this," cried the nurse. As they were taking Juliet to the Capulet family tomb, Romeo heard of her death. Alas, the messenger of Friar Laurence hadn't gotten to him in time. Romeo bought poison and rushed to Verona to Juliet's tomb. In the tomb, he met Paris, and Paris, thinking Romeo was there to do mischief, drew his sword. Romeo was forced to kill Paris, who begged with his last breath, "If you are merciful, open the tomb and lay me with Juliet." Romeo did that and then, laying himself beside Juliet, took the poison. "Eyes, look your last! Arms, take your last embrace! and lips, oh, you the doors of breath, seal with a kiss, and thus with a kiss I die." Just as Romeo died, Juliet awoke and, in horror, saw her still warm but dead husband. "What's here? A cup, closed in my own true love's hand? Poison, I see. Oh! and you've drunk all and left no friendly drop to help me after? I will kiss your lips. Maybe some poison yet is there. No! I hear a noise. Then I will be brief." She grabbed Romeo's dagger and said, "Oh happy dagger! This is your home, here rust and let me die!" and she stabbed herself and fell on her beloved Romeo and died. The guards and soon the parents of Romeo and Juliet came. Friar Laurence explained what had happened, and they all realized what horror their old hatreds had brought. The families embraced and promised to never hate again. "A gloomy peace this morning with it brings . . . we must go to have more talk of these sad things. Some shall be pardoned, and some punished . . . for never was story of more woe than this of Juliet and her Romeo."

Checking Your Comprehension

After reading this story once, what do you think the answers to these questions are? It's OK to guess, and it's OK to not know the answers yet.

1. Why are the Capulets and Montagues enemies?
2. Why is Romeo banished?
3. How does Romeo die?
4. How does Juliet die?

Be a Vocabulary Detective

Working in pairs, look for hints and guess the vocabulary from the context clues. Then fill in the blanks with the correct answers.

Clue 1

The Capulets and Montagues were *sworn* enemies of each other. Romeo Montague knew he was *forbidden* to enter the house of the Capulets, so he wore a disguise.

1. *Sworn* is _____ (adj).
   a) totally so   b) bad words   c) like a large knife

2. *Forbidden* is _____ (adj).
   a) allowed   b) not allowed   c) not remembered

Clue 2

Romeo and Juliet were *star-crossed* lovers. They *fell head over heels in love* with each other, and that led to their story of *woe*.

3. *Star-crossed* is _____ (adj).
   a) loving the sky   b) fated to have problems   c) able to choose

4. To *fall head over heels in love* means _____ (idiom/v).
   a) to immediately   b) to trip   c) to hurt oneself
      be in love

5. *Woe* is _____ (n).
   a) a great sadness   b) a great happiness   c) a sickness

Clue 3

After Romeo killed Tybalt he was *banished* to *yonder* Mantua. He ran to the *monastery* to ask Friar Laurence for advice.

6. To be *banished* is to be _____ (adj).
    a) put in prison   b) made to disappear   c) sent away

7. *Yonder* is _____ (adj).
    a) here   b) over there   c) not old

8. A *monastery* is _____ (n).
    a) a place where   b) a large hill   c) a town
        monks live

Clue 4

When the nurse thought Juliet was dead she said it was as if the cold *frost* had killed a lovely flower. When Juliet awoke in her *tomb,* she saw that Romeo was dead and grabbed his *dagger,* telling the dagger to stay in her chest forever and *rust* there.

9. *Frost* is _____ (n).
    a) the beginning   b) icy cold   c) diseased

10. A *tomb* is _____ (n).
    a) a large grave   b) part of the hand   c) a bed

11. A *dagger* is _____ (n).
    a) poison   b) a small, sharp knife   c) a gun

12. *Rust* is _____ (n).
    a) a reddish brown,   b) relaxed   c) disappear
        powdery substance
        on metal

Questions for Discussion

First, reread the story carefully, looking for the deeper meanings and reviewing the vocabulary. Then in small groups discuss the following questions with your classmates. Be sure to tell what your native culture is.

1. What was your favorite sentence in this story and why?
2. How could you change the story to prevent the tragedy so that Romeo and Juliet could have lived happily ever after?
3. This story is very similar to the Greek myth of Pyramus (peer-a-muss) and Thisbe (thiz-bee), two lovers whose parents hate each other and who die tragically like Romeo and Juliet. (They are to meet at night in the forest. A lion tears off Thisbe's coat and she runs away. Pyramus comes, finds the coat,

thinks Thisbe has been eaten by the lion, and kills himself. When Thisbe returns she finds her darling dead. She takes his knife and kills herself.) This theme of tragic "star-crossed" lovers is universal and is found in many cultures. Is there a similar story in your culture? Share it with the class.

Finding the Moral/Lesson

In small groups look at the following proverbs and decide which of these proverbs best fits the lesson of this story. Then share your answer with the class.

a. Love conquers all.
b. The course of true love never did run smooth.
c. Let sleeping dogs lie.

Now, turn to page 196, find the moral in your list of proverbs, and check it off. Can you think of any other proverbs that will fit the moral?

Double-checking the Vocabulary

Fill in the crossword with the following vocabulary words: sworn, forbidden, star-crossed, head over heels, woe, banished, yonder, monastery, frost, tomb, dagger, rust.

Across

3. a weather condition in which the temperature goes below freezing
4. fated, a life decided by destiny
5. a large enclosed space for a dead person
7. a small sharp knife used as a weapon
9. a large building where monks and friars live
11. complete, with no possibility of change

Down

1. a reddish brown powdery substance found on old metal
2. an idiom to describe falling in love
3. absolutely not allowed
6. sent away as a punishment
8. over there
10. great, intense sadness

Building Vocabulary from Shakespeare

From this story we get the following modern expressions:

1. a Romeo (This now means a romantic man who loves many women.)
2. star-crossed

Be sure to turn to page 207 and add these idioms to your mythology and legends word list.

Cultural Notes: In the United States people generally try to judge people not by their family or by their name, but as individuals and for their own selfworth. America was founded on the values of independence and self-determination. The Declaration of Independence states that all humans are created with the rights to life, liberty, and the pursuit of their own happiness. To judge someone by family or social status takes away each person's freedom to determine his or her own life by his or her own work and ideas.

Writing

Think, *in English,* about these cultural values and then, in correct American form and as briefly as possible, discuss the similarities or differences of these values with values in your culture.

Speaking

Share your ideas about these values with the class.

Part **4**

Endings

Now this is not the end.
It is not even the beginning of the end.
It is perhaps, the end of the beginning.
—Winston Churchill, speech, 1942

List of Proverbs

This is a list of the proverbs found in your book. They are listed in alphabetical order. Look for the one you have chosen as the best moral or lesson of each story, read the "definition" (in italics) to be sure you understand the proverb, and then make a check mark (✓) by that proverb. When you have finished this book, you will have checked twenty-four proverbs. Following this list, on page 199, you will find other common proverbs. This will give you a dictionary of over one hundred well-known American English proverbs.

1. Absence makes the heart grow fonder. *You like someone or something better when that person or thing is far away.*

2. Actions speak louder than words. *You can tell how a person truly feels by what he or she does, not by what that individual says.*

3. All that glitters is not gold. *Some things appear to be very valuable, but they are really not.*

4. All things come to him [her] who waits. *Be patient and you will eventually get what you want.*

5. All work and no play makes Jack a dull boy. *It is not healthy for someone to work all the time and not relax.*

6. All's fair in love and war. *During a war or when you are in love, it's OK to do anything to get what you want.*

7. Beggars can't be choosers. *If you ask for something, you can't complain when you get it and then you don't like it.*

8. Better late than never. *It's better to do something late than to not have done it at all.*

9. Better safe than sorry. *It's better to be careful and not take risks that could lead to unhappiness.*

10. The bigger they are, the harder they fall. *When famous people fail, their failure is very dramatic and shocking.*

11. A bird in the hand is worth two in the bush. *Having something for certain is better than trying to get something that might be better.*

12. The course of true love never did run smooth. *When you are in love you expect perfect happiness, but you will have difficult times.*

13. Curiosity killed the cat. *Curiosity can get you into trouble, especially if you are curious about someone's private life.*

14. Do unto others as you would have others do unto you. *Treat others the way you would like them to treat you: This is called the Golden Rule.*

15. Don't bite off more than you can chew. *Don't take on more responsibility than you can handle.*

16. Don't burn your bridges until they are crossed. *Don't destroy friendships or possibilities you might need for later.*

17. Don't count your chickens until they're hatched. *Don't make plans on the results of something until it actually happens.*

18. Don't cry over spilt milk. *If a mistake has been made and can't be changed, it doesn't help to feel badly about it.*

19. Don't judge a man until you've walked in his shoes. *Don't criticize someone until you have had the same experiences.*

20. Don't look a gift horse in the mouth. *Don't complain about a gift that has been given to you.*

21. The early bird catches the worm. *If you wake up and get to work early, you will be successful—also, this is like, first come first served.*

22. A fool and his money are soon parted. *Foolish people waste their money.*

23. Fool me once, shame on you; fool me twice, shame on me. *If someone has tricked you once, be careful of being tricked again; the second time, it will be your fault.*

24. Forewarned is forearmed. *You can prepare for something when you know what to expect.*

25. A friend in need is a friend indeed. *A true friend is one who will help you when you are in trouble.*

26. The grass is always greener on the other side. *Someone else's life or situation always looks more attractive than what you have.*

27. A half a loaf is better than none. *Getting only part of what you want is better than getting nothing at all.*

28. Haste makes waste. *If you do your job too quickly, you will make many mistakes and not succeed.*

29. He who laughs last, laughs best. *If someone is happy because he or she has hurt another or done something bad, the person who gets revenge on the one that did the bad thing will be the happiest one.*

30. Honesty's the best policy. *It's always a good idea to tell the truth.*

31. Hope springs eternal in the human breast. *No matter what tragedies occur, human beings will always be able to hope.*

32. If at first you don't succeed, try, try again. *Keep trying to reach your goal; don't give up.*

33. If wishes were horses, beggars would ride. *Hoping for something doesn't make it come true.*

34. If you can't beat them, join them. *If you can't defeat your enemies, join them.*

35. If you play with fire, you will get burnt. *If you do something dangerous, you will get hurt.*

36. It is more blessed to give than to receive. *Giving things is more rewarding than getting things.*

37. It is never too late to say you are sorry. *An apology is always better than ignoring the problem.*

38. It was the straw that broke the camel's back. *When someone has many problems, one more problem, however small, will cause that person to finally lose control.*

39. Leave well enough alone. *If something works well, don't try to improve it. Another proverb is, If it's not broken, don't fix it.*

40. Let sleeping dogs lie. *If a situation could be dangerous, let it alone.*

41. Look before you leap. *Consider all parts of a situation before you make a decision.*

42. Love conquers all. *Love is the strongest power.*

43. Make hay while the sun shines. *Take advantage of an opportunity when it is there.*

44. Marry in haste, repent at leisure. *If you make the wrong decision in who you marry, you will suffer the consequences for your whole life.*

45. Might makes right. *The stronger one will win.*

46. Misery loves company. *Unhappy people like to be with each other and talk about how horrible they feel.*

47. Moderation in all things. *Never go to extremes in what you do.*

48. Never lie to your minister, doctor, or lawyer. *Always tell the truth to people whose help you need.*

49. No pain, no gain. *Nothing can be accomplished without hard work.*

50. Nothing hurts like the truth. *Often the truth is painful.*

51. Nothing ventured, nothing gained. *Nothing can be accomplished if you don't try.*

52. One good turn deserves another. *If someone does you a favor, you must do a favor for him or her.*

53. Out of sight, out of mind. *If you don't see something or someone frequently, you will forget about it.*

54. Out of the frying pan into the fire. *Going from a bad situation into an even worse situation.*

55. Patience is a virtue. *It is good and rewarding to be patient.*

56. Pride goes before a fall. *If you are too proud of yourself, it will cause you to fail.*

57. Seeing is believing. *Don't trust what people say; find out if it is true by experience.*

58. Silence is golden. *Not talking too much is valuable.*

59. Slow and steady wins the race. *If you continue to work slowly and carefully, you will be more successful than if you try to do the job fast but not with care.*

60. A stitch in time saves nine. *If you fix a small problem right away, it will not become bigger later.*

61. There's a time for work and a time for play. *There is a right time to do work and a right time to relax and don't mix them up.*

62. There's always a light at the end of the tunnel. *Even in the most difficult of situations there will be hope at the end.*

63. There's no place like home. *A person is happiest with what is most familiar.*

64. Three can keep a secret, if two of them are dead. *No one can be trusted to not tell a secret except the person who the secret is about.*

65. Truth is stranger than fiction. *Things that really happen are harder to believe than stories people invent.*

66. Two wrongs don't make a right. *Maybe someone else did something bad and didn't get punished, but that doesn't mean it's OK for you to do something bad.*

67. In unity there is strength. *A group of people with the same goals can accomplish more than individuals.*

68. A watched pot never boils. *Something you want to happen will not happen while you are concentrating on it.*

69. When it rains, it pours. *Good or bad things seem to happen in large numbers all at once.*

70. Where there's smoke, there's fire. *When there is some evidence of a problem, there probably is a problem.*

71. You can't have your cake and eat it too. *You can't enjoy the benefits of two conflicting things.*

72. You reap what you sow. *Whatever you do you will pay the consequences for your actions.*

These proverbs were not choices in the stories, but they are very well known in everyday American conversations.

73. An apple a day keeps the doctor away. *If you eat an apple every day you will stay healthy.*

74. The apple doesn't fall far from the tree. *Children are very similar to their parents.*

75. Bad news travels fast. *Reports of misfortunes are quickly repeated.*

76. Birds of a feather flock together. *Similar people associate with each other.*

77. Don't close the barn door after the horse is stolen. *It doesn't help to fix a problem after the problem has occurred.*

78. Don't cross that bridge till you come to it. *Don't worry about something that hasn't happened yet.*

79. Don't put off for tomorrow what you can do today. *Don't procrastinate—do what you need to do when you need to do it.*

80. Don't put the cart before the horse. *Be sure to always do things in the correct order.*

81. Don't throw the baby out with the bath water. *Don't discard something valuable just because it's associated with something you want to get rid of.*

82. If looks could kill, I'd be dead. *You look like you are really angry with me.*

83. If the shoe fits, wear it. *This refers to an unflattering remark that you must accept because it is true.*

84. If you can't stand the heat, get out of the kitchen. *If you feel that a situation is too difficult for you, you should stop complaining and just leave the situation.*

85. It's like looking for a needle in a haystack. *It is an impossible task and cannot be successful.*

86. It's never too late to learn. *You can learn something new, and change your opinions, as long as you are alive.*

87. It takes two to tango. *When two people work together as a team, they both share the responsibilities.*

88. It's the pot calling the kettle black. *You shouldn't criticize someone else for having a fault that you have.*

89. Laugh and the world laughs with you; cry and you cry alone. *When you are happy you will be surrounded by friends, but when you are sad, people will avoid you.*

90. Like father, like son. *Children often follow the examples of their parents.*

91. A little bird told me. *When you heard something but you don't want anyone to know the source (who told you).*

92. Man does not live by bread alone. *In order to survive, humans need more than material things; they need positive emotions like love, and they need friends, family, etc.*

93. A man's home is his castle. *You can do whatever you want to do in your own house.*

94. A man is known by the company he keeps. *You can guess what a person is like by his or her friends.*

95. Money doesn't grow on trees. *Making money doesn't come easily.*

96. No news is good news. *If you don't hear from someone, you can assume that everything is OK.*

97. Nothing succeeds like success. *If you have succeeded in the past, you will succeed in the future.*

98. A penny for your thoughts! *I want to know what you are thinking about.*

99. A picture's worth a thousand words. *Pictures convey information faster and better than words.*

100. A rolling stone gathers no moss. *If you don't settle down, you will not be attached to anything: This could be positive or negative depending on the opinion of the speaker.*

101. There's more than one way to skin a cat. *There are many different ways to accomplish a goal.*

102. Those who live in glass houses shouldn't throw stones. *Don't criticize someone for the same faults as yours.*

Additional Activities and Themes for Writing and Discussion

Now that you've finished reading these stories, you must have noticed a surprising repetition of similar themes.

Identify the common themes and then compare and contrast them. You can do this in small group discussions, in writing, or in a presentation to the whole class. You could present a play, or you could have a trial. Here are a few suggestions to get you started.

Common Themes

You Can't Escape Your Fate
    Theseus and the Minotaur
    Hercules
    King Arthur and His Knights of the Round Table
    Oedipus the King

You Have Been Warned . . . You Have Free Choice
    The Little Boy Who Cried Wolf
    Pandora's Box
    Minerva and Arachne
    Daedalus and Icarus
    Cupid and Psyche
    Orpheus and Eurydice
    The Trojan War (Achilles)

Pride Goes before a Fall
    The Fox and the Grapes
    The Fox and the Crow
    The Hare and the Tortoise
    Minerva and Arachne
    Echo and Narcissus
    Daedalus and Icarus
    The Trojan War (Achilles)

Patience Is a Virtue
    The Goose and the Golden Egg
    Orpheus and Eurydice
    The Odyssey
    Cupid and Psyche

Love Hurts
   Echo and Narcissus
   Ceres and Proserpine
   Orpheus and Eurydice
   Hercules
   Theseus and the Minotaur
   Oedipus the King
   King Arthur and His Knights of the Round Table
   Romeo and Juliet

Good Triumphs over Evil
   The Hare and the Tortoise
   The Ant and the Grasshopper
   Ceres and Proserpine
   Cupid and Psyche
   The Odyssey
   Lady Godiva

Evil Finally Triumphs over Good
   Pandora's Box
   Hercules
   The Legend of Robin Hood
   King Arthur and His Knights of the Round Table

Possessions Hidden under Stones
   King Arthur and His Knights of the Round Table (Arthur) (Galahad)
   Theseus and the Minotaur

Possible Trials

Have your class select a judge, a lawyer for the defense, and a lawyer for the prosecution, then choose a jury of twelve people and witnesses and defendants. The lawyers will state the case, and the jury will decide the verdict: guilty or not guilty. For example:

   Is Peeping Tom guilty of spying?
   Is Launcelot guilty for the fall of Camelot?
   Is Hercules guilty of the murder of his wife and children?
   Is Deianira guilty of the murder of Hercules?
   Should Theseus pay alimony to Ariadne?
   Is the sheriff of Nottingham guilty of unfair harassment of Robin Hood?
   Is Robin Hood guilty of theft?

Additional Activities

As previously stated, these stories form a foundation of American language, vocabulary, and culture and are therefore referred to in everyday adult conversation. Keep your eyes and ears open and try to gather vocabulary, proverbs, and any references to these stories and fables from newspaper cartoons, television and radio announcements, billboards, songs, conversations, advice columns, etc. You'll be surprised at how many words and proverbs you can find in just one week. You could have a contest and see who can find the most. Eureka! You will discover more and more English and culture every single day.

Future Readings

If you would like to read more fables, myths, and legends *now*, go to your public library (or local bookstore) and ask the librarian (or bookseller) to help recommend these types of stories found in the "juvenile" section. There are hundreds of wonderful books that retell these famous stories in reading levels that will be easy and enjoyable for you. Don't forget to read the books and look at the videos suggested in the background notes of each reading selection.

The following is a small list of famous collections of fables, myths, and legends taken or translated from the original sources. They are probably in an English too advanced for you at this time; but when you are fluent, give them a try.

Aesop's Fables, by Arthur Rackham
By Jove! Brush Up Your Mythology, by Michael Macrone
From Achilles Heel to Zeus's Shield, by Dale Corey Dibbley
King Arthur and His Knights of the Round Table, by Roger Lancelyn Green
Mythology: Timeless Tales of Gods and Heroes, by Edith Hamilton
Tales of Troy and Greece, by Andrew Lang
The Collected Works of William Shakespeare
The Illustrated Dictionary of Greek and Roman Mythology, by Michael Stapleton
The Merry Adventures of Robin Hood, by Howard Pyle
The Age of Fable, by Thomas Bulfinch
The Stories of the Greeks, by Rex Warner

Appendix: Mythology and Legends Word List

Fill in this list as you learn new words. You should indicate the page or the story each word is from, the part of speech, the meaning; add whatever will help you to remember the word. Then be sure to look for these words in everyday conversation.

1. Neptune   p. 40   planet   n.

2. Pluto   p. 40   planet   n.

3. Venus   p. 40   planet   n.

4. chronology   arrangement of events

5. chronicle   record of historical events

6. chronic   long lasting

7.

8.

9.

10.

11.

12.

13.

14.

15.

16.

17.

18.

19.

20.

21.

22.

23.

24.

25.

26.

27.

28.

29.

30.

31.

32.

33.

34.

35.

36.

37.

38.

39.

40.

41.

42.

43.

44.

45.

46.

47.

48.

49.

50.

51.

52.

53.

54.

55.

56.

57.

58.

59.

60.

61.

62.

63.

64.

65.

66.

67.

68.

69.

70.

71.

72.

73.

74.

75.

76.

77.

78.

79.

80.

81.

82.

83.

84.

85.